Interviews with **George F. Kennan**

Conversations with Public Intellectuals Series
Douglas Brinkley and David Oshinsky, General Editors

Interviews with

George F. Kennan

Edited by
T. Christopher
Jespersen

University Press of Mississippi
Jackson

www.upress.state.ms.us

Photograph on page iii courtesy of Special Collections, Princeton University Libraries

10   09   08   07   06   05   04   03   02   4   3   2   1
⊗
Library of Congress Cataloging-in-Publication Data

Kennan, George Frost, 1904–
     Interviews with George F. Kennan / edited by T. Christopher Jespersen.
        p.   cm. — (Conversations with public intellectuals series)
     Includes index.
     ISBN 1-57806-448-1 (cloth : alk. paper) — ISBN 1-57806-449-X (pbk. : alk. paper)
        1. Kennan, George Frost, 1904– —Interviews.   2. Kennan, George Frost, 1904–
—Political and social views.   3. Ambassadors—United States—Interviews.   4. Historians—
United States—Interviews.   5. United States—Foreign relations—1945–1989.   6. United
States—Foreign relations—Philosophy.   7. United States—Foreign relations—Soviet Union.
8. Soviet Union—Foreign relations—United States.   9. Cold War—Diplomatic history.
10. United States—Civilization—1945–   I. Jespersen, T. Christopher, 1961–   II. Title.
III. Series.

E748.K374 A3   2002
327.73'0092—dc21   2001057507

British Library Cataloging-in-Publication Data available

Books by George F. Kennan

American Diplomacy: 1900–1950. Chicago: University of Chicago Press, 1951.

An American Family: The Kennans—The First Three Generations. New York: W. W. Norton, 2000.

Around the Cragged Hill: A Personal and Political Philosophy. New York: W. W. Norton, 1993.

At Century's Ending: Reflections, 1982–1995. New York: W. W. Norton, 1996.

The Decline of Bismark's European Order. Princeton: Princeton University Press, 1979.

Kennan et al. *Encounters with Kennan: The Great Debate*. London: Frank Cass, 1979.

The Fateful Alliance: France, Russia, and the Coming of the First World War. New York: Pantheon, 1984.

From Prague after Munich: Diplomatic Papers, 1938–1940. Princeton: Princeton University Press, 1968.

Memoirs, 1925–1950. Boston: Little, Brown and Company, 1967.

Memoirs, 1950–1963. Boston: Little, Brown and Company, 1972.

The Nuclear Delusion: Soviet-American Relations in the Atomic Age. New York: Pantheon, 1983.

Realities of American Foreign Policy. Princeton: Princeton University Press, 1954.

Russia and the West under Lenin and Stalin. Boston: Little, Brown and Company, 1960.

Sketches from a Life. New York: Pantheon, 1989.

Soviet-American Relations, 1917–1920, Vol. I: *Russian Leaves the War*. Princeton: Princeton University Press, 1956.

Soviet-American Relations, 1917–1920, Vol. II: *The Decision to Intervene*. Princeton: Princeton University Press, 1958.

Contents

Introduction

George F. Kennan is America's most famous diplomat. He achieved that status over fifty years ago and has held it ever since, an impressive feat of longevity, especially considering that he never once served in the nation's highest diplomatic post, secretary of state. He did serve in various other positions, starting with third secretary in Moscow for Ambassador William C. Bullitt after the United States normalized relations with the Soviet Union in 1933 and continuing with Bullitt's successor, Joseph E. Davies, until 1938, though he spent most of 1935 in Austria recuperating from ulcers. He transferred to Prague, Czechoslovakia, in the fall just as Western European leaders signed the infamous Munich agreement with Adolf Hitler, permitting the Nazi occupation of Czechoslovakia's German-speaking region as part of an effort to appease the dictator. A few months later, Hitler swallowed up the rest of the country. Kennan moved to Berlin as first secretary from 1939 until Germany declared war on the United States in December 1941. After a few months of Nazi internment, he transferred to Lisbon, Portugal, where he became counselor and later chargé d'affaires. He returned to Moscow in 1944 as deputy chief of the mission, second only to Ambassador W. Averell Harriman himself. After the war, he became deputy for foreign affairs at the newly-created National War College in 1946 and then returned to the State Department as the first director of the also newly-created Policy Planning Staff from 1947 to the end of 1949. Finally, he served twice as ambassador, the first time to the Soviet Union very briefly in 1952, the second time to Yugoslavia from 1961 to 1963. His two tenures as ambassador do not stand out from other ambassadorial appointments in the nation's history, except perhaps for his first assignment where he managed to get himself declared *persona non grata* by Moscow shortly after taking over the post. In public comments, he compared his short time as ambassador in the Soviet Union to the period he spent confined by the Nazis, and Soviet Premier Joseph Stalin took exception. Eleven years later, Kennan resigned his ambassadorship to Yugoslavia because of a dispute with Congress over trade policy, leading one scholar to judge his two ambassadorial stints as failures.[1] In short, George Kennan's stature did not arise from the positions he held, nor has it been sustained by his service in the nation's diplomatic corps.

Kennan achieved his standing because of what he wrote. In a sense, Kennan has been the nation's premier diplomatic intellectual. After his time at the Policy Planning Staff, and in between and after his ambassadorial appointments, Kennan wrote articles and books and lectured from his position at Princeton University's Institute for Advanced Study. His reputation, however, began its rapid ascent earlier with one aptly titled "long" telegram he, as chargé d'affaires, transmitted from Moscow to Washington after the war. Prior to that, Kennan had almost resigned, frustrated over his ineffectiveness in influencing policy toward the Soviet Union. In his own words, all he had done up until that point was "little else but pluck people's sleeves, trying to make them understand the nature of the phenomenon with which we in the Moscow embassy were daily confronted and which our government and people had to learn to understand if they were to have any chance of coping successfully with the problems of the postwar world."[2]

In February 1946, and from his sickbed no less, Kennan finally had his chance. Averell Harriman had resigned as ambassador, and his replacement, Walter Bedell Smith, had not yet arrived. As the one in charge of the embassy, Kennan was asked in early February to relay his thoughts on Soviet policies in light of recent speeches by Stalin and a few other high-ranking officials. In his response, which ran to 5,540 words, Kennan explained at the outset that the questions involved were "so intricate, so delicate, so strange to our form of thought, and so important to analysis of our international environment that I cannot compress answers into [a] single brief message without yielding to what I feel would be [a] dangerous degree of oversimplification."[3] He apologized "for this burdening of telegraphic channel," but insisted that such a lengthy exposition was needed because the issues were so critically important. He then proceeded to lay out a five-part explanation of "(1) Basic features of post-war Soviet outlook. (2) Background of this outlook. (3) Its projection in practical policy on official level. (4) Its projection on unofficial level. (5) Practical deductions from standpoint of US policy."[4]

Kennan offered a description of Soviet policy, its historical dimensions, and the psychological and sociological underpinnings to Soviet leaders' thinking in what Anders Stephanson has called "one of the two or three most important texts of the early cold war."[5] With its dramatic portrayal of the Soviet leadership and its discussion of the rising likelihood of conflict between the United States and Soviet Union, Kennan's telegram captured and made tangible the bits and pieces of information, suspicion, and supposition that had been floating around Washington for some time. Even though what he wrote did more to crystallize, rather than influence, the growing mood amongst American policymakers, its impact was substantial just the same. Kennan characterized it as "nothing less than sensational." Walter Isaacson and Evan Thomas have pointed out that "[w]hat made the Long Telegram so immensely influential was not what Kennan said . . . but what Washington was willing to hear."[6] Kennan suggested that the timing of his telegram appeared to have been critical. "Six months earlier this message would probably have been received in the Department of State with raised eyebrows and lips of disapproval. Six months later, it would probably have sounded redundant, a sort of preaching to the convinced."[7]

Why were policymakers willing to listen to Kennan in February 1946 but not earlier? With his ascension to the presidency in April 1945, Harry S. Truman began changing course from Franklin D. Roosevelt, at first gradually, then more noticeably, in the nation's dealings with the Soviet Union. The wartime cooperation engendered in the "Big Three" (President Roosevelt, British Prime Minister Winston Churchill, and Stalin) and the notion of Four Policemen (the United States, Great Britain, the Soviet Union plus China in Asia), both collaborative concepts for postwar engagement and cooperation stressed by FDR, gave way to increasing wariness and even hostility in viewing Soviet actions in Eastern Europe and Iran toward the end of 1945 and into 1946.[8]

By February, when Kennan was asked to comment on Russian leaders' speeches around the time of the elections for the Supreme Soviet, policymaking attitudes in the United States had hardened considerably from the year before. Kennan's long telegram, therefore, did not so much change perceptions or awaken individuals to the nature of Soviet power as much as it reinforced prevailing wisdom for some within the Truman administration. "It was one of those moments when official Washington," Kennan wrote in his memoirs, "was ready to receive a given message."[9] Not only that, but Kennan managed to describe Soviet actions and intentions in highly dramatic, even emotionally charged, language, a real bonus when the time later came for the administration to take its case for action to the American public.

Kennan's assessment of the highly favorable and widespread reception his telegram received exaggerates things a bit. Although Kennan wrote in his memoirs that he believed President Truman had read his telegram, Deborah Larson has pointed out that there is no evidence to indicate this.[10] She even asserted that Kennan's telegram did not greatly impress Secretary of State James Byrnes, at least not to the point of changing his thinking about the Soviet Union.

Kennan's writing did greatly impress one influential person, however, and that was Secretary of the Navy James Forrestal, who had the telegram reproduced and distributed widely because "it was exactly the kind of job for which [he] had looked vainly elsewhere in the government."[11] Forrestal's critical role in promoting the long telegram (and by association its author by having him brought back to Washington in April 1946 for a position at the National War College), and especially having it transformed from a State Department missive into a publication for the July 1947 issue of *Foreign Affairs*, led one historian to ask who the real author of the article truly was.[12]

A good question, for Kennan's "Sources of Soviet Conduct," published initially with the author listed only as "X," came just months after President Truman's call for $400 million in assistance to Greece and Turkey as the most effective means of opposing Soviet interference in the region. The "X" article served as an intellectual justification for what became the nation's policy of containment. In describing the Soviet leaders' efforts to sow relentless division within the capitalist world, Kennan put forth a couple of caveats in the best sense of President Woodrow Wilson, who in his various public appeals during World War I made sure to distinguish between the German leadership, which he deemed evil, and the German people, in whom he had much confidence. Likewise, Kennan argued that whatever the beliefs articulated by Soviet leaders, their thinking did "not represent [the] natural outlook of [the] Russian people." Russians were "friendly to the outside world" and were basically "eager above all to live in peace and enjoy fruits of their own labor."[13] The problem came from the Soviet leadership and the official party line, which itself was "not based on any objective analysis of situation beyond Russia's borders; that it has, indeed, little to do with conditions outside of Russia; that it arises mainly from basic inner-Russian necessities which existed before recent war and exist today."[14]

Kennan described the view from the Kremlin as "neurotic," reflecting the "traditional and instinctive Russian sense of insecurity." The Russian leaders were fearful because of the relative backwardness of their society in comparison with the West. They understood the precariousness of their rule, which was "relatively archaic in form, fragile and artificial in its psychological foundation, unable to stand comparison or contact with political systems of Western countries."[15] Indeed, Kennan explicitly wrote about Soviet leaders' worries of "foreign penetration." In highlighting the language Kennan employed in forwarding his opinions, Frank Costigliola has convincingly demonstrated that Kennan's syntax revealed much about his own thinking and fit neatly with contemporary popular attitudes about gendered imagery and stereotypes prevalent in American society at the time. That is partly why it struck such a responsive chord with policymakers and was subsequently used to bolster the administration's public assertions that a more aggressive strategy was needed to counter Soviet actions. As Costigliola makes abundantly clear, this analysis was far from the presumed "realist" or "realistic" assessment of Soviet intentions and capabilities.[16] And Kennan continued to use that kind of language even when he reconsidered the "X" article with the benefit of twenty years' hindsight. In his memoirs, Kennan wrote that what he really wanted to accomplish with the "X" article was to convince Western leaders that however impressive Soviet leaders may have appeared, they "were not supermen." What, then, to do? "Stand up to them, I urged, *manfully* but not aggressively, and give the hand of time a chance to work."[17]

In detailing events leading up to the publication of the "X" article, Kennan indicated that all he really sought to accomplish was to draw up a blueprint for "handling this problem—a way that offered reasonable prospects of success, at least in the sense of avoiding a new world disaster and leaving the Western community of nations no worse off than it then was." Specifically, he wanted the West to stop making what he saw as unilateral concessions, and he laid the groundwork for resistance to Soviet leaders' continual efforts to extend their political influence. In the end, this policy of firm, vigilant containment would allow time for Moscow's internal contradictions "to moderate Soviet ambitions and behavior."[18]

Kennan's dichotomy between the people and leadership and his faith in the Russian people ran into difficulties in the "X" article, particularly when he employed some potent imagery. The Soviets' "particular brand of fanaticism, *unmodified by any of the Anglo-Saxon traditions of compromise,* was too fierce and too jealous to envisage any permanent sharing of power."[19] Not having benefited from the Anglo-Saxon "traditions of compromise," which were not named but which perhaps started with the Magna Carta and continued with the Glorious Revolution, the Act of Union in 1707, and the Reform Bills of 1832, 1867, and so on, all of which addressed issues of law, political participation, and accountability, the Soviets fell into a different world, one that drew on Russia's geographical expanse.[20] Having both an Asian and European presence, the Soviet Union was a conduit for the transmission of ideas and qualities from one area to the other. In this specific case, there was reason to worry. Kennan unwittingly drew on Asian stereotypes fresh from the war in the Pacific. "From the Russian-Asiatic world out of which they had emerged they carried with them a skepticism as to the possibilities of permanent and peaceful coexistence of rival forces."[21] His Russians, at one point, are in danger of slipping backwards in something of a reverse social-Darwinian process straight from the nineteenth-century schools of racial hierarchy that accompanied Western colonialism. Kennan's impressions of Chinese, for example, were not particularly high. He would later write that they "seemed to be lacking in two attributes of the Western-Christian mentality: the capacity for pity and the sense of sin."[22]

Kennan went further. Members of the Soviet leadership were unquenchable in their drive for absolute control, which Kennan defined as having to reach a position of "unchallengeable" security. In "seeking that security of their own rule," he insisted, the Soviets "were prepared to recognize no restrictions, *either of God or man,* on the character of their methods."[23]

In the end, Kennan did not simply describe and analyze Soviet behavior; he also prescribed diplomatic medication for what ailed Western nations. What made Kennan's writing so crucial for American foreign policymaking in this instance, as John Lewis Gaddis has aptly pointed out, was both his ability to capture policymakers' convictions and the elusiveness of the language he selected, the latter of which also accounts for the sizeable number of scholars who have written about him subsequently. Although not decisive "in shaping the Truman administration's approach to the world," Kennan, through the ideas he articulated in his writings, "more than anyone else, did provide the intellectual rationale upon which" the containment doctrine was founded.[24] After having laid down the foundation of Soviet diplomacy, Kennan called for an American policy based on "a long-term, patient but firm and vigilant containment of Russian expansive tendencies."[25] This is what the Truman administration had in mind when it proposed the Truman Doctrine to Congress, calling for military aid to Greece and Turkey in 1947, and it was this policy of containment for dealing with the Soviet Union that would be followed by successive administrations, Democratic and Republican alike, over the next forty-plus years.

What did Kennan mean, however, by "firm and vigilant containment" and what did he mean when he wrote in the "X" article of needing to practice "the adroit and vigilant application of counter-force at a series of constantly shifting geographical and political points, corresponding to the shifts and manoeuvres of Soviet policy"?[26] Members of the Truman administration came to interpret these phrases differently from what Kennan would later claim had been his intent. Indeed, in writing about the "X" article in his memoirs, Kennan admitted that it had several serious deficiencies, one of which was "the failure to make clear that what I was talking about when I mentioned the containment of Soviet power was not the containment by military means of a military threat, but the political containment of a political threat."[27] Citing the same phrases quoted above, Kennan conceded that the language "was at best ambiguous, and lent itself to misinterpretation."[28] In the end, what ended up happening to Kennan's article, according to Gaddis, was that "rhetoric overleaped intent by a considerable degree."[29]

Kennan came to argue against the aggressive policies adopted by the Truman administration, but he had cautioned Washington from the beginning. In his long telegram, for example, he had warned that "the greatest danger that can befall us in coping with this problem of Soviet communism is that we allow ourselves to become like those with whom we are coping."[30] Finding himself and his ideas less highly regarded by key policymakers, he decided to leave the Policy Planning Staff at the end of 1949. His successor, Paul Nitze, made explicit what some had thought was implicit in the "X" article: namely, that the United States had to fashion a fundamentally military response to

Soviet aggression. Nitze's most famous piece of writing on this subject came in the form of National Security Council document number sixty-eight, or NSC-68 for short. Although not much different from what the Truman administration had been pursuing since 1947, according to Melvyn Leffler, NSC-68 did make abundantly clear the need for increased spending on military matters, from military assistance programs to other nations to the country's national defense budget, to the point where it actually called for raising taxes and decreasing spending on social programs.[31]

Kennan would serve briefly as ambassador to the Soviet Union in 1952, but that ended badly, and he resigned from the Foreign Service in 1953 after an awkward experience with the new secretary of state, John Foster Dulles, over his exact status. He later accepted the offer from the Kennedy administration to serve as ambassador to Yugoslavia, but two years later, he decided to resign after Congress passed trade legislation he thought unfairly penalized that country and undermined his standing with the Belgrade government.

In the interviews that follow, Kennan is asked to comment on a range of issues, all in his capacity as an expert on the Soviet Union. In the first interview, with conservative reporter Joseph Alsop in the fall of 1956, Kennan discusses events in Eastern Europe, particularly Poland and Hungary, both of which were experiencing popular discontent over Soviet policies. Nikita Khrushchev decided to let the Poles handle their own affairs, but on November 4, the Red Army moved into Hungary in response to the government's decision to withdraw from the Warsaw Pact. Khrushchev's ultimate actions remained unknown to Kennan when he spoke with Alsop, but the brutal suppression demonstrated two things: first, that even with Stalin's death, the Kremlin was not going to allow Eastern European governments to pursue an independent line. Second, when the United States did nothing in response, it manifested the emptiness of the Eisenhower administration's rhetorical call for liberation of those peoples under Soviet control. In assessing the circumstances, Kennan insists that "Americans must also learn to base our calculations and hope on long-term realities of human nature and political behavior, not on the short-term ones."

The second interview occurred in 1960 and was done with Melvin Lasky, who asks Kennan to comment on the state of literature and social commentary in the Soviet Union and the West. Lasky focuses on Soviet criticisms of Kennan's own historical writings, and both lament what Kennan terms the lack of "a more genuine critical literature with higher standards" in the West. He cites the writings from the twenties as examples of less commercial, more positive, and more beautiful writing. Kennan also comments on the deleterious impact of the automobile on Western society, especially when compared with earlier times: "It must fragmentise and explode that which has been united," leading him to conclude, "we have succeeded in disintegrating the American community to an absolutely appalling degree." He mourns this decline in community, and, although not a Luddite, he casts doubts on the development of new technologies just for the purpose of saving labor or "speeding-up of the processes of production or daily life."

His concern about an increasingly fragmented American society was not new. The importance of unity was a theme he had raised in his "X" article, where he wrote that without it, the West could not respond effectively to the Soviet challenge. In 1947, Americans had a unique opportunity to unite and welcome "the responsibilities of moral and political leadership that history plainly intended them to bear."[32] In 1960, Kennan was still worried about some of the same problems facing the West, and he also included some new ones, like environmental degradation from nuclear testing, the "reckless exhaustion of natural resources," and "the fetish of growth in the qualitative sense." Four decades later, Americans are still grappling with unrestrained suburban growth and the fragmentation caused by relying on the automobile in cities like Atlanta, Houston, Phoenix, and Los Angeles, to name a few. And with cars increasingly giving way to ever-larger sport utility vehicles, Kennan's warnings about environmental degradation and resource depletion remain as trenchant as ever.

In the next two interviews, the first with Robert Moskin for the *Saturday Evening Post* in 1963, shortly after he had resigned his position as ambassador to Yugoslavia over disagreements with the nation's policy (but before President Kennedy's assassination), and the second with Louis Fischer, as part of the oral history project at the John F. Kennedy Presidential Library, Kennan discusses his frustrations with Congress's involvement in the foreign policy process, and how the individual jealousies of representatives and senators work against the nation's interests. Kennan decided to step down because he was frustrated with the Congressional decision to cut off most-favored-nation status to communist countries, including Yugoslavia, without regard for Yugoslavia's independent path under the leadership of Josip Broz Tito. Kennan argued that such simple-mindedness in policymaking failed to appreciate the substantial differences amongst communist countries. Like his other comments, these concerns about Congressional involvement in the process of making foreign policy continue to resonate. Presidents and their chief foreign policymakers have to grapple with the prickliness and idiosyncracies of senators and representatives without respect to time period or party affiliation.

Kennan's interview with Richard Challener focuses on his relationship with President Eisenhower's secretary of state, which is quite natural since the interview was conducted for the John Foster Dulles oral history project at the Seely Mudd Manuscript Library at Princeton University. One major topic of discussion is the manner in which Kennan retired from the Foreign Service.[33] Also of interest is how, even in discussing Dulles, Kennan raises the issue of deferring to Congress and how the secretary did it too much. "He stuck very close to the grass roots—what was possible with Congress. And I just wasn't brought up that way. I was brought up in the Executive Branch of government. It's a different thing."

The next interview is a twenty-five-year retrospective on the "X" article. Kennan discusses how the U.S.-Soviet relationship looks in light of changes in the international community since his famous article was published in 1947, and he returns to some of the same themes—"deeply-rooted traits in Soviet psychology"—that animated his original concerns. Soviet leaders continue to engage in the deliberate misuse of the truth, Kennan asserts, to the point that he wonders whether they had not destroyed their own ability to "distinguish truth from falsehood." Their continuing "hysterical preoccupation with espionage" and insulting references to Americans as "imperialists" and "monopolists" leads Kennan to warn against Americans engaging "in unreal hopes for intimacy with either the Soviet regime or the Soviet population."

In the interview with Eric Sevareid, conducted in September 1975, Kennan again returns to the issues of containment, his thinking at the time he wrote the "X" article, and the state of America's relations with the Soviet Union. When queried about his preference for an earlier diplomatic era, specifically the eighteenth century, Kennan is also asked to respond to the accusation of being an elitist. "Well, of course, I am. What do people expect? God forbid that we should be without an elite." Sevareid also returns to some of Kennan's earlier concerns about interference from Congress in the process of making foreign policy.

The final two interviews, both short pieces for *U.S. News & World Report*, were conducted in 1982 and in 1996, the latter when Kennan was ninety-two years old. In the first interview, nuclear weapons are discussed in light of the Reagan administration's build-up, and Kennan has much to say about the administration's refusal to renounce using nuclear weapons first. In the second interview, containment is raised, once again, but this time the interviewer, Jeff Trimble, asks about policies in light of the vast changes that had swept over the Soviet Union, now Russia, during the past ten years. Kennan offers his opposition to the expansion of NATO on the grounds that it will inflame Russian nationalism, and in returning to something he had spoken about with Melvin Lasky three and a half decades earlier, he asserts that the two main problems facing the United States are "the world environmental crisis" and "bringing nuclear weaponry and the weapons of mass destruction under control." He concludes with the admonition that "Washington needs a house-cleaning" because of how the nation's "diplomatic apparatus" has become so "vastly overbureaucratized."

In one sense, Kennan's last interview in this volume speaks to the major theme of his conversations, and much of his writing, over the past half century: namely, the need for Americans to dedicate themselves to the international problems they face. Although known as a Russian expert, Kennan frequently used his discussions about Russia and its people to reflect on the United States and its people. Whether it was calling for Washington to put forth "a much more positive and constructive picture of [the] sort of world we would like to see," in the long telegram; whether it was inveighing in the "X" article for Americans to accept "the responsibilities of moral and political leadership that history plainly intended them to bear"; or whether it was his most recent call for Americans to keep "relations with the rest of the world on an even keel," Kennan has often served as the nation's diplomatic conscience, and he has used the Russian people and their political leadership as mirrors through which to scrutinize America's policies and, in the process, hold the United States to a higher set of expectations.[34]

This collection of interviews does not constitute every one George F. Kennan has given over the years, especially if his many times of speaking before

Congress are considered as a type of interview. There have been others, but they were not included because of space limitations. In addition, Kennan has published so many books, including a recent account of his ancestors, that it is obviously well advised for anyone interested in his career to consult his writings, especially his two volumes of memoirs.

The value of these unedited interviews, like most interviews, is the opportunity to examine carefully what George Kennan says, both as indications of (perhaps) less guarded utterances by the very nature of the interview process itself and as a point of comparison with what Kennan has written. It is also useful to consider Kennan's remarks over the years particularly on the changing nature of America's involvement in world affairs from the mid-to-late 1940s, when he was catapulted to prominence, to the mid seventies and the end of the nation's involvement in Southeast Asia, and finally up to the present. It was the logic of containment that propelled the United States into Vietnam, in opposition to the expansion of communism into this region, and as part of the "counterforce" articulated by Kennan in his "X" article. Should Kennan, however, really shoulder such blame for what others inferred from his writing, but what, he later wrote, was never his intention? Or should he have known better and taken greater care in his original phrasing?

Either way, there is obvious value in reading for the first time, or rereading, what he has said over the years, about the nature of U.S.-Soviet relations, about Soviet society and its political leadership, about the Russian people, and about Americans, their society, and its mechanisms for conducting foreign policy. Kennan is an astute observer. In 1956, he noted to Joseph Alsop, "I believe some day Russia will have to abandon East Germany and let it rejoin Germany." Thirty-three years later, Kennan's prophecy came true as the Berlin Wall collapsed, and the Soviet leadership chose not to respond with the kind of force it had used in Hungary. Of course, Kennan had no way of knowing how long it would take before German unification came about, and he was always careful when discussing the timing of changes he thought would eventually come to Eastern Europe or the Soviet Union.

Like others, policymakers or academics, Kennan was affected by the forces, events, developments, and individuals that shaped the unfolding of history while he has lived. His interviews speak in more ways than one to the complexities, nuances, and intrigues of his personality as well as to the times in which he has lived. And it is for those reasons that it is worth considering what this eminent diplomatic intellectual has had to say over the years.

In the process of collecting the interviews, selecting which ones to include, and writing up the introduction, I have benefited from the assistance of a number of people, and I would like to take this opportunity to thank them for their assistance.

I need to begin by thanking George F. Kennan for granting permission to use two of the interviews as well as the cover photograph. Thanks go to Terrie Bramley and Harriet Wasserman for their help with the permissions, and to Chris Andayo at CBS News, Susan LeClair at *U.S. News & World Report*, Steven C. Pettinga with the *Saturday Evening Post*, and Jessica Whipple at *Foreign Policy*. Chris Kitto at the Mudd Library was especially helpful on the pictures. Kara Drake at the Kennedy Library processed my request to declassify small portions from that interview, though some of it still remains closed. Anders Stephanson gave me the citation for the interview with Eric Sevareid, and Matthew Mucher discovered and copied a number of the interviews. As always, Theresa gave helpful suggestions, especially on the introduction.

At the University Press of Mississippi, Seetha Srinivasan provided me with helpful guidance at critical points. She was also very patient with my efforts to meander through the permissions maze. Walter Biggins gently prodded me by checking on my progress from time to time. I am grateful for the opportunity to participate in the series on conversations with public intellectuals, and I would like to thank David Oshinsky for the recommendation.

Finally, I should provide a short explanation on the dedication. George F. Kennan, as I argue in the introduction, is America's most famous diplomat, and yet his fame really arises from what he has written over the years more than his actions while in the nation's foreign service. He has been regarded as both a diplomat and a scholar. In that vein, I had the good fortune to work with three individuals who, like Kennan, have served, or continue to serve, their countries in diplomatic posts, and who, again like Kennan, are all scholars in their own right.

I thus dedicate this book to my former colleague at Clark Atlanta University, and friend, Cedric Grant, who served as Guyana's ambassador to Zambia, Great Britain, and the United Nations and whose writings on the Caribbean are widely recognized and highly regarded; to Lawrence Pope, who served as

the U.S. ambassador to Chad and who spent a year as the diplomat-in-residence at Clark Atlanta University, where I taught for seven years, and whose expertise, cogency, and bristling wit made him a delightful presence; and to William Stanton, whose Ph.D. in literature certainly makes him one of the best read of the members of the nation's diplomatic service, and whose remarks on academics and U.S.-China relations will always make me think carefully before speaking. To all three go my thanks, gratitude, and respect.
TCJ

Notes

1. David Mayers, *George F. Kennan and the Dilemmas of US Foreign Policy* (New York: Oxford University Press, 1988), 215.

2. George F. Kennan, *Memoirs, 1925–1950* (Boston: Little, Brown and Company, 1967), 293.

3. Telegram, 22 February 1946, Kennan to Secretary of State, *Foreign Relations of the United States 1946* vol. VI (Washington: Government Printing Office, 1969), 676. Hereafter cited simply as telegram. Some sources have put the number of words at 8,000. It was long, but not that long.

4. Ibid.

5. Anders Stephanson *Kennan and the Art of Foreign Policy* (Cambridge: Harvard University Press, 1989), 45.

6. Walter Isaacson and Evan Thomas, *The Wise Men: Six Friends and the World They Made, Acheson, Bohlen, Harriman, Kennan, Lovett, McCloy* (New York: Simon and Schuster, 1986), 354.

7. Kennan, *Memoirs, 1925–1950*, 295.

8. Melvyn P. Leffer has a very good discussion of this period in his *A Preponderance of Power: National Security, the Truman Administration, and the Cold War* (Stanford: Stanford University Press, 1992).

9. Ibid., 294.

10. Kennan, *Memoirs, 1925–1950*, 294. Deborah Welch Larson, *Origins of Containment: A Psychological Explanation* (Princeton, N.J.: Princeton University Press, 1985), 257.

11. Walter Millis, ed., *The Forrestal Diaries* (New York: The Viking Press, 1951), 136.

12. Lloyd C. Gardner, *Architects of Illusion: Men and Ideas in American Foreign Policy, 1941–1949* (Chicago: Quadrangle Books, 1970), 270–300. Although *Foreign Affairs* listed "X" as the author of "The Sources of Soviet Conduct", it was fairly quickly known in Washington that Kennan was the name behind the letter.

13. Telegram, 698.

14. Ibid., 699.

15. Ibid.

16. Frank Costilgiola, " 'Unceasing Pressure for Penetration': Gender, Pathology, and Emotion in George Kennan's Formation of the Cold War," *Journal of American History* 83 (March 1997), 1309–39.

17. Kennan, *Memoirs, 1925–1950*, 364. Emphasis mine.

18. Ibid.

19. X, "The Sources of Soviet Conduct," *Foreign Affairs* 25 (July 1947), 568. Emphasis mine. The "X" article was also reprinted in *Foreign Affairs* (Summer 1987), 852–68. All quotes are from the 1947 issue.

20. Kennan evidently took great pride in his exclusively "Anglo-Saxon" family heritage. See Mayers, 16.

21. X, "The Sources of Soviet Conduct," 568.

22. George F. Kennan, *Memoirs, 1950–1963* (Boston: Little, Brown and Company, 1972), 56.

23. X, "The Sources of Soviet Conduct," 569.

24. John Lewis Gaddis, *Strategies of Containment: A Critical Appraisal of Postwar American National Security Policy* (New York: Oxford University Press, 1982), 26.

25. X, 575.

26. Ibid., 576.

27. Kennan, *Memoirs, 1925–1950*, 358.

28. Ibid., 359.

29. Gaddis, 65.

30. Telegram, 709. For an excellent analysis on what the United States did become, see Stephen J. Whitfield, *The Culture of the Cold War* (Baltimore, The Johns Hopkins University Press, 1991).

31. Leffler, 355–57.

32. Kennan, 1947 edition, 582.

33. For another account, see Kennan, *Memoirs, 1950–1963*, 168–89.

34. Telegram, 708; "Sources of Soviet Conduct," 582.

Chronology

1904	George Frost Kennan is born on February 16 in Milwaukee, Wisconsin, to Kossuth and Florence Kennan.
1921–1925	Kennan attends and graduates from Princeton University.
1926	In September, Kennan enters the Foreign Service.
1928	Kennan begins special Russian training in Germany, Estonia, and Latvia.
1933	In November, United States establishes formal diplomatic relations with the Soviet Union.
1933	In December, Kennan accompanies Ambassador William C. Bullitt to Moscow as an interpreter.
1934	Kennan serves as third secretary in Moscow.
1935	Kennan recuperates from ulcers in Vienna and serves as second secretary.
1935	In November, Kennan returns to Moscow as second secretary under Ambassador Joseph E. Davies.
1937	In October, Kennan comes back to Washington on the Soviet desk in the State Department.
1938	In September, Munich agreement between Germany, Italy, France, and England allows Germany to occupy a portion of Czechoslovakia. Kennan becomes second secretary in Prague, Czechoslovakia.
1939	In March, Germany occupies the remainder of Czechoslovakia.
1939	In September, Germany invades Poland. Kennan moves to Berlin as second secretary, and later becomes first secretary.
1941	In December, Germany declares war on the United States. Kennan interned by Germans.

1942   In June, Kennan returns to Washington.

1942   In September, Kennan becomes counselor in Lisbon, Portugal, and later chargé d'affairs.

1944   In January, Kennan joins European Advisory Commission in London, England. In June, Allied forces invade France. In July, Kennan returns to Moscow as chargé d'affairs.

1945   In April, President Franklin D. Roosevelt dies; Harry Truman becomes president. In May, Germany surrenders.

1946   In February, Kennan sends "long" telegram. In April, Kennan returns to Washington to become deputy commandant for foreign affairs at the National War College.

1947   In March, President Truman proclaims the Truman doctrine and asks Congress for $400 million in assistance to Greece and Turkey. In May, Kennan moves to Policy Planning Staff in the State Department. In July, *Foreign Affairs* publishes "The Sources of Soviet Conduct," by Kennan under the pseudonym "X."

1949   In December, Kennan leaves Policy Planning Staff.

1950   In January, Kennan takes leave of absence from the Foreign Service to join the Institute for Advanced Study at Princeton University. In April, NSC-68. In June, North Korea invades South Korea.

1952   From April to October, Kennan serves as U.S. ambassador to the Soviet Union. (Kennan's official termination as ambassador came in March 1953, but since he was declared persona non grata in October, that date has been listed.)

1953   In June, Kennan retires from Foreign Service.

1956   In November, Soviet Union invades Hungary.

1957   Kennan gives Reith Lectures on the BBC.

1957–58   Kennan becomes Visiting Professor, Balliol College, Oxford University.

1961   Kennan becomes U.S. ambassador to Yugoslavia.

1963   Kennan resigns as ambassador to Yugoslavia.

1967   Kennan publishes first volume of his memoirs.

1972   Kennan publishes second volume of his memoirs.

1974–present Kennan is professor emeritus at the Institute for Advanced Study.

Interviews with **George F. Kennan**

The Soviet Will Never Recover

Joseph Alsop / 1956

From *Saturday Evening Post*, 24 November 1956.
Reprinted by permission.

ALSOP: *George, let me start by asking why you think your lonely prophecy of 1945, of an eventual breakaway from the Soviets in Eastern Europe, is being so dramatically fulfilled today?*

KENNAN: Well, it's the kind of question that has to be answered by beginning at the beginning. And to begin with, Russian statesmen, long before the Soviet era, have always tried to establish Russian domination over the peoples of Eastern Europe: and they've always run into trouble. The Eastern European peoples have always had a higher standard of living than the mass of the Russian people and they have also been much further advanced in constitutional liberties and personal freedom. Therefore, if the Russian leaders granted these peoples their accustomed liberties and standard of life, they were granting them more than they dared grant to the people of Russia. But if they did the opposite, this was not good enough for the peoples of Eastern Europe. This has been one basic reason for the Russian failures in this region—both the failures in Czarist times and this great setback the Kremlin has now met with.

That is the first cause. As to the second cause, you may think me naïve, but I believe that the second cause is the plain fact that the Soviet communist system is deeply wrong—wrong about human nature, wrong about how the world really works, wrong about the importance of moral forces, wrong in its whole outlook. For this reason I have always doubted whether the Soviet system would ultimately survive in full totalitarian form even in Russia itself, where it has so obstinately survived until now. And I think that this thesis of mine has been proved in these vast and stirring developments in Poland and Hungary and throughout Eastern Europe.

There's one other practical factor that should also be noted. Because of their subjection to the Soviet Union, these great erstwhile food-producing areas of Eastern Europe today face serious food deficits. This is a shameful fact. And I note that in Poland and Hungary, where the trouble burst forth, an hour's hard work is reported to buy even less bread than in the other Eastern European countries.

But, of course, the chief reasons why the trouble has come just now, at this particular moment, lie in the death of Stalin and the things that have happened since Stalin's death.

ALSOP: *But I also gather you think there would have been a blowup sometime, even if Stalin's successors had maintained a fully Stalinist system?*
KENNAN: If his successors had maintained a fully Stalinist system, I still think this would have broken down in Eastern Europe eventually, because it was contrary to human nature. But it was certainly the death of Stalin and the change in spirit and method on the part of his successors that produced the great changes at this juncture.

ALSOP: *In that connection, one of the things that have most interested me is the strong surge of patriotism and even of anti-Soviet feeling that appears to have occurred within the ranks of the official Communist parties in Eastern Europe. That seems to confirm your thesis too.*
KENNAN: On that point, Joe, we must be careful not to be confused. Two separate and distinct processes are involved in the recent great events. One of these processes we might describe as the fight for national freedom, for freedom from Soviet control. In this native fight communists have joined enthusiastically. The other process we might describe as the fight for personal freedom, for personal liberties, for constitutional guaranties of representative government and of civil rights. This process is anticommunist; it comes from the mass of the people, and most communists oppose it in part at least—even the communists who want freedom from Kremlin domination. These two struggles should not be confused; they do not necessarily always go together.

ALSOP: *Yet in Poland, for instance, hasn't Gomulka already gone very far in the promises that he has made to his people? He's promised a return to peasant agriculture, restoration of free speech and discussion, and even some freedom in the forthcoming election. And isn't this, in a sense, a rather slippery slope for Gomulka?*

KENNAN: He will run risks, certainly, if he grants too much personal freedom. Yet Gomulka has another important factor on his side. At the end of the last war, Poland was literally moved several hundred miles to the west. Thus Poland's new western borders are not going to be readily acceptable to the German people. They cut very far into what has traditionally been purely German territory. Unless some means can be found to settle this difference between the Germans and the Poles over the western borders, it seems to me that the Poles are always going to be dependent to some extent on the Russians for the guaranty of their present frontiers. That means they must think a long time before installing an actively anticommunist government, which is the alternative to Gomulka. In considering the future of these governments in Eastern Europe, in short, each must be treated as a special case. Each will be influenced, in the way all nations are influenced, by its own national situation. All the same, I don't think it impossible that the Communist parties of Eastern Europe, and outstandingly the Polish party, may really someday move in the direction of real democracy.

ALSOP: *But do you think the Kremlin can grant substantive national independence to one or two or three of its satellites without, in the end, being forced to release all Eastern Europe from its grip?*

KENNAN: As I see it, the events our people have been following with such desperate attention mark a perhaps decisive historic turning point. Their consequences will be profound, and they will affect practically every portion of the world which is today subjected to Soviet power or exposed to Soviet influence. In particular, to answer your question, I think that the recent developments in Poland and Hungary are bound, sooner or later—and I don't predict the timing—to mark the end of Moscow's abnormal power and domination throughout all of Eastern Europe. The same fundamental forces are plainly at work throughout the whole area.

ALSOP: *But will the people in the Kremlin really permit this kind of enormous breakaway from their authority without using force on the largest scale? After all, they've already used their tanks against the unarmed Hungarian workers!*

KENNAN: Well, there are undoubtedly some leaders in Moscow who long to use the entire power of the Red Army, if need be, in order to crush this drive for independence everywhere. But there are two excellent reasons why I think they are unlikely to do this. First, they cannot easily restore Stalinist repression in the satellites without restoring it in Russia. Second, the physical problem has become almost insoluble for them. The satellite armies and police have been shown to be unreliable. They have, in fact, joined the patriots in a good many cases. So what are the Soviets to do—place a tank in every street in every satellite country? That was the difficulty, as I believe, that saved Tito from attack by the Red Army when he proclaimed his independence. You can be sure Stalin would have liked to drink Tito's blood. But Stalin also had enough prudence to see that there was no Yugoslav whom he could depend upon to help him rule Yugoslavia. And he did not want to place a Soviet tank in every street in Belgrade and Zagreb.

ALSOP: *But do you positively rule out a resort to brute force by the Kremlin?*
KENNAN: Certainly not. Obviously, the Soviet leaders may be goaded into extreme measures by unwise Western action, maybe even by unwise Western gloating. More important still, they may be goaded by the threat that in Eastern Europe they will not just have independent governments allied to Russia, but instead will get actively anti-Soviet and anticommunist governments. For this reason, I think that in this Eastern European area they'll also go to great lengths to avoid withdrawing their occupying forces altogether. This is a tricky business, and it can take any sort of turn between this moment, when we sit talking here, and that moment in the future when our words will be printed. But on the whole, barring tragic accidents, I don't think extreme measures will be used by the Kremlin throughout the whole area. Hungary is, of course, still the great question mark as we talk today.

ALSOP: *Well then, George, let us return to the tremendous process at work in the satellite states. You said just now that the same fundamental forces were at work throughout the whole area of Eastern Europe which is the Soviet Union's primary buffer area. But how do you analyze these forces? Take the youth, all of whom were supposed to be devoutly indoctrinated communists, until these same young people appeared in the forefront of the patriot bands. How do you explain this seeming contradiction?*
KENNAN: Of course some of the young people were communist-indoctrinated, and perhaps, before Stalin died, some of these indoctrinated young people were the toughest and most ambitious of the youth. They were fascinated and

intoxicated by the gigantic, seemingly monolithic false front of Stalinist Russia's power. But these, I am sure, were always a small minority. Young people, after all, have to live and to enjoy life, to do the things that other young people do. The communists monopolized all the organizational frameworks in which the life of youth could take place. And if, let us say, young people wanted to march and sing, or take an excursion into the country, or go on a camping trip, the only way they could march and sing or do these other things was in a communist organization. But that did not alter their inner feelings about communism. In general, I think that in the satellite countries not more than five percent of the people were ever on the side of Russian rule, and that includes the youth.

ALSOP: *What do you feel about the reports that we have so often heard about the really volcanic effect on the youth and the workers' groups, on the communist party rank and file, and even on the hard core, of the circulation of Khrushchev's famous speech denouncing Stalin?*
KENNAN: That was surely of great significance. Like the youth leaders I mentioned, many other hard-core communists really believed in Stalinism prior to the circulation of Khrushchev's speech. They believed in Stalinism in a rather determined, bitter, pragmatic way. Their discipline was so great, their communist training so impressive, that their attitude of belief at least intimidated and impressed those others who did not believe. But the true believers were just the ones who were hardest hit by Khrushchev's speech on Stalin. Here was confirmation of what other people had been trying to tell them for twenty to thirty years—namely, that the communist movement in Russia had been captured by a single man; that it had been most cynically and terribly used to serve his ambitions and his fears and his sense of guilt. And as soon as they saw this, I think these believing Eastern European communists succumbed to great and growing despair and confusion and uncertainty, and this could not fail to communicate itself to people around them.

ALSOP: *And this started the ferment?*
KENNAN: Yes, one must remember that in none of these Eastern European countries was Russian rule at all welcome or at all easy to take. These are all proud peoples. They all are conscious of the ability to govern themselves if they are let alone. They feel—even most of those who are communists have

always felt—that they ought to be free of the humiliating domination by Moscow.

ALSOP: *That leads to another question that has been puzzling me. Do you think the Soviet leaders were at all prepared for what has now happened? I've been amazed by all the hasty journeys by top members of the Soviet presidium—like Suslov's and Mikoyan's successive trips to Budapest, first to save Rakosi; then, when that failed, to install Geroe; and then, when Geroe fell, to give their blessing to Nagy. And surely that last-minute trip of Khrushchev, Molotov and the others to Warsaw, taking with them nothing but the most empty threats, looked like a desperate improvisation?*

KENNAN: Certainly there was some miscalculation on the part of the present Soviet leaders. It looks as though they had not understood at all how unpopular Russian rule was in Eastern Europe, how miserable people were, how deep was the bitterness and the desire for independence. They thought after Stalin died that all they had to do was relax this pressure a little bit and people would be happy and grateful, and all would be well. They never realized how terribly tightly the spring had been compressed and what impetus it would get if you loosened it a bit. You can see in the record of these past three years the gradual stages of their awakening to this. Sometimes, they have relaxed and then, in a rather panicky way, have tried to tighten up again. You remember that Nagy was in power once before in Hungary, but, for some reason or other, he must have frightened them. They must have felt that Nagy was going too far—so they put Rakosi back in. And that didn't work either. One might almost say about the question you asked me a few moments ago—whether they could reimpose Stalinism—that this has already been tried and has failed.

ALSOP: *Putting Rakosi back didn't work, as I understand it, largely because his own Hungarian communist leadership turned against him. But how do these communists just under the top—these people who are influential enough to make trouble—suddenly get the idea that Rakosi ought to go, for instance, and that someone else should come in who has been in prison or in exile?*

KENNAN: Well, first of all, there must have been grave pressures on the economic front; certainly there is great distress of mind among these communists about the failure to meet the economic plans. In a simple, practical way, that failure raises difficult questions of responsibility among them as to who is at fault. Then, too, economic failure promotes another phenomenon which bothers the communist leaders a great deal, and that is lack of political enthusiasm. They don't like the feeling that they don't really command the hearts of the people. Now you can say, why do they worry about this, being as ruthless as they no doubt are? Well, for instance, there are very practical reasons why they should worry about the new generation of the youth growing up in opposition to the regime. After all, the youth must provide the needed new recruits for the governmental bureaucracy, the Communist Party, the secret police. The communist leaders don't dare to recruit people who are unreliable.

ALSOP: *You mean they cannot make the system work if their recruits are limited to the time servers, the prostitutes and the blockheads?*
KENNAN: Very well put. And it goes further than that. Even the tough, able, convinced, senior communists begin to lose their prestige with the population. And soon you get a situation where the communists who are stationed in a small town or village, or even in a fair-sized city, find themselves very lonely because they are up against a sort of unspoken conspiracy involving everyone else.

ALSOP: *In effect, they are put into Coventry.*
KENNAN: They are put into Coventry, and yet no one does anything for which he can really be easily punished. It is simply that the collective farm doesn't work, the grain doesn't come onto the market, the production of the factory isn't very good and young people hang back, they show no desire to take positions of responsibility in the communist youth movement and the Communist Party. And this goes from bad to worse, until even the hard-core believers get worried and begin to argue about what could be done about it. Then they look across the border at Tito and they begin to say, "Well, what we should do is to get Rakosi out of here. He's an old Stalinist; he's more beholden to the Russians than he is to the Hungarian people; and the people know it. Let's get someone who really cares about Hungary, at any rate, at the top of the party. Then we may have some enthusiasm, some confidence and some production again."

ALSOP: *What's so striking, George, is that everything that you have been saying about the causes of the events in Hungary and Poland would seem to me to apply with equal force in all the other satellites. But how about the effect of this kind of development in Eastern Europe on the Communist parties in the rest of the world?*

KENNAN: Well, I think regardless of the way the dust finally settles, the things that have happened in Poland and the disorders that have broken out in Hungary—this whole sequence of events—really spells the end of what one might still call the Third International. The monopolistic position of Russia, of Moscow, as the single center of inspiration and discipline for the communist movement had already been badly shaken even before the recent great events. Now an enormous impetus has been given to the disintegration of Moscow's authority. In fact, I would hazard the guess that Moscow's position of ascendancy is already at an end. After this, there will be no central communist leadership— not only for ideology but also for world policy.

ALSOP: *This end of Moscow's position as the communist Vatican is certainly an enormous change, which is bound to have enormous consequences. But, George, we still haven't tackled the most interesting problem that is raised by the satellite ferment. What do you think will be the effects within Russia?*

KENNAN: One must always be cautious in these matters, but if past history of the Russian communist movement is any guide, I should think that someone would have to suffer for this really striking Soviet reverse.

ALSOP: *Who do you think that would be?*

KENNAN: It's necessarily only a guess, but I would think that the person who would be most blamed for all this would be Khrushchev. I shall be surprised if this crisis does not end by affecting his position in the Communist Party. Of course, all the members of the Soviet presidium today share the guilt for the state of affairs in Eastern Europe. The old Stalinists share it outstandingly, because it was Stalin's regime which produced these impossible conditions and made some such reaction as has now occurred quite inevitable in the long run. But Khrushchev and the others must share it, too, because they have sponsored the relaxations of recent years, and these relaxations have helped to release disorder at this particular juncture. And probably Khrushchev and Bulganin and the rest will bear the immediate brunt.

ALSOP: *You haven't left many of the Soviet political leaders much of a leg to stand on. I know you think the Red Army's power has greatly increased since Stalin died. Do you think Marshal Zhukov will be the beneficiary if Khrushchev loses his top place?*

KENNAN: It is very dangerous to speculate on these things, on the basis of what we know today. We know that the army leaders were extremely miserable under Stalin's rule, that Stalin treated them very badly, and Zhukov, in particular. We know that Stalin humiliated them, gave them no credit for the very genuine military achievements which they had registered during World War II, and in general made them feel discontented and frustrated. It's quite evident, too, that the position of the army has become much more important since Stalin's death, not only because of the fact that he is gone but because of the relative change in the position of the Soviet secret police. Stalin really ruled the country through the secret police. Now that the secret police have been hamstrung, the position of the army has become relatively much more important, simply because every dictatorial regime has to have some armed sanction for its power. Today that sanction is provided by the army in the Soviet Union.

ALSOP: *And, as I understand it, you also feel that Zhukov, the key man in the army, dislikes both Malenkov and Khrushchev.*
KENNAN: I have no idea about his personal feelings, of course. But I do have the impression that he is not politically particularly close to Khrushchev, and I would think it's even less likely that he's close to Malenkov.

ALSOP: *Malenkov having been Stalin's chief henchman at the time that Zhukov was humiliated?*
KENNAN: That's correct. And therefore I'm inclined—and again this is only a guess—to think that the army's influence will not be fully identified with either of the existing factions in the leadership. Yet I don't think, either, that the army as an institution will attempt to take overt political responsibility. Finally, we must remember that almost all the existing Soviet leaders have been on the job for a very long time. There must someday be a breakthrough of younger forces, younger personalities. It must indeed be rather near at hand. And that is what I really look for. Yet I can't possibly tell exactly what these new personalities will be like, if they, in fact, emerge at all in the near future.

ALSOP: *We have no idea who they are, have we?*
KENNAN: Scarcely any. Yet strong personalities, natural future leaders, must exist in ample numbers in the ranks of the party, the bureaucracy and the new industrial management.

ALSOP: *But what will these new leaders mean, if they emerge? In brief, do you think that the events in Eastern Europe will have a shaking effect on Russia's internal situation? Or to put it even more extremely, do you think the character of the Soviet Government may change?*

KENNAN: I think the internal character of the Russian Government has already been altered by the end of Stalinism and by the greater dependence of the present leaders as a group on certain important elements in Soviet society.

ALSOP: *You mean they now have to have a kind of popular support?*
KENNAN: They have to have a kind of popular support—not a support by the broad masses of the people, but by groups like the army, the party bureaucracy, the industrial managers and the intelligentsia. Now all these groups are bound to have their ideas affected by the blowup in Eastern Europe. The writers and artists and professors and other intellectuals will be the hardest hit by it, because by my observation these people have managed to retain, even through the Stalin era, a certain sort of underlying idealism and self-respect and hope that Russia would prove to be a good force and not a bad force in the world affairs. They've already suffered great discouragements, and this is going to be another terrible discouragement for them, just when hope was dawning again. Then, too, the effect on Russian student youth is going to be very great. Altogether, I wouldn't preclude the possibility that you might even get repercussions within Russia.

ALSOP: *You mean actual disaffection in the near future?*
KENNAN: Well, I used the word repercussions. I cannot tell what form they will take. But I am sure events such as those we have witnessed in Hungary in these past days are bound to have an unsettling effect on many people in these influential Soviet groups. In this sense, you might use the term disaffection.

ALSOP: *But, if you believe there is a serious possibility—even a slim possibility—of this kind of thing in Russia, why, then, do you think that a return to Stalinism is so improbable? I should have thought the least hint of internal disaffection would have triggered a new ruthlessness in Moscow.*
KENNAN: But there are two difficulties about a return to Stalinism. First, one person would have to be acknowledged as the new Stalin, and second, this man would need to have the qualities that Stalin had. Neither of those difficulties can be easily overcome today. Most of the present Soviet leaders, if they are agreed on any one thing, are agreed that they do not want a repetition of the conditions they knew under Stalin. Molotov, who had a curious doglike loyalty to his old chief and seems to have admired his ways, is a probable exception. They wanted the post-Stalin relaxation even before Sta-

lin's death. It is not something that they were pushed into. They wanted the relaxation for very personal reasons, among other reasons because they were in some ways the chief sufferers under Stalin. They were the ones whose comfort, peace of mind and security were most endangered by Stalin's terrible way of running the country. So they will hardly agree on choosing a new Stalin. Furthermore, whom could they choose? In my judgment, none of them is capable of running Russia the way Stalin did. He was a man of unique gifts and of unique evil. It took this combination to run any country the terrible way Stalin ran Russia. No, the last thing the present leaders want is the return of the nightmare of the last years of Stalin.

ALSOP: *We are already beginning to hear claims that our American efforts have had much responsibility for the great change in Eastern Europe. If the consequences in the Soviet Union are as you say, the claims will be even louder. What do you think of them?*
KENNAN: If you are talking about direct efforts on our part—if you mean this was the result of something we were doing—then the best answer I can make is to tell you the Russian fable about the fly that rode all day on the nose of the ox. When the work in the fields was over and the ox returned to the village in the evening, the fly saluted the villagers with great pride and said to them, "We've been plowing." But if you mean that the example of free life in America and elsewhere was an important inspiration to the Hungarians, then I can go along completely. It seems to me that the kind of claim you repeated diminishes and tarnishes the grandeur of these events. And these events do have grandeur, very great grandeur, because they are visible proof that certain principles, certain moral principles, really must be observed in the long run in the successful government of great peoples. These events prove that if those principles are consistently violated over a long period of time, this violation avenges itself. It inevitably produces trouble and disorder and even greater violence and bloodshed and tragedy. The Soviet Government has ignored these principles, has denied these principles, for a very long time indeed; and they are getting the results of that in Eastern Europe today. After long years of patient suffering, the peoples of the satellites are reacting, very valiantly reacting, against the treatment they have been subjected to.

ALSOP: *In short, you're arguing, George, that evil in government brings its own reward.*
KENNAN: It brings its own reward. This is my deepest belief. There are great truths in this world about human nature that have to be observed if govern-

ment is going to be successful. We in America did not create those truths. I only think we were informed of some of them by the founding fathers of our country and, to some extent, we have remembered them. And to the extent that we stick with them ourselves and have confidence in them, we shall at least have a great power of example. Let us not inflate our claim beyond that point. If, as I had long and desperately hoped, greater freedom is coming to Eastern Europe, it is coming because there are, after all, healthy forces in all peoples, and those forces are now asserting themselves. We didn't create those forces. They were there. God created them, in my opinion.

ALSOP: *But what about the operation of these great truths, these profound principles of yours, in the Soviet Union itself?*
KENNAN: You mean, why have they not seemed to operate thus far? The answer to that, I think, is not the efficiency of the Soviet system, but the previous poverty and ignorance of large portions of the Russian people. History teaches us that when peoples are very poor and very ignorant, they may be subjected for very long periods of time to the most ruthless despotism. It is only when they begin to sense the possibility of better and higher things that they begin to demand better and higher things. And it is precisely because Russia has undoubtedly made great progress in many spheres, because Russia has raised the level of the people's life in fact, that conditions have now been created in which it's going to be remarkably difficult to rule the Russian people ever again as Joe Stalin ruled them.

ALSOP: *What would you say were the most important of these new conditions—the spread of education, for example?*
KENNAN: I think I would. They cannot avoid educating their people, otherwise they cannot have a good managerial class or even a good industrial-foreman class. But such people must have self-respect. They must have hope. They cannot be indefinitely submitted to cruel humiliations.

ALSOP: *And that means you can't have Stalin's kind of totalitarian rule without as a minimum risking the loss of everything that has been gained in Russia?*
KENNAN: It means that, and more than that. The present leaders of the Soviet Union are now caught in perhaps their deepest dilemma. This dilemma lies in the growing disparity between the reality of the governmental pattern they have inherited from Stalin and Lenin, and the reality of the Russia in which

they live today, the more educated, more literate and more highly organized Russia that they have created by their industrialization. Between these two realities, something is going to have to give somewhere. The Russian rulers are going to have to recognize—and recognize at home—certain of these basic truths about human nature which have been so nobly demonstrated in Eastern Europe. When that time will come or how it will come, I don't know.

ALSOP: *But you feel sure it will come.*
KENNAN: Yes, I feel sure it will come. You may ask whether it will mean the breakup of the present communist leadership. Again, I don't know. I have said on other occasions that freedom might come to Russia by erosion from despotism rather than by the violent upthrust of liberty. When you get very serious disagreements in a society such as the communist society in Russia today, they can, of course, always be composed by a regrouping of forces among the top, the most influential people; and in such a regrouping popular aspirations may well find their reflection. But if these divisions are not so composed, they can quite suddenly and unpredictably lead to the most staggering internal difficulties and weaknesses. That has not happened in Russia so far, but it is a possibility that should not be excluded. What we have seen in Hungary and in Poland in these recent days, could conceivably be the beginning of a disintegration which will carry deep into Russia itself. It could be the prelude to a great convulsion in the whole Soviet communist system. Or perhaps it may be the prelude of bad trouble in special areas, like the former Baltic states and the Ukraine. We must wait and see.

ALSOP: *Yet, on the whole, you don't think that's really likely at the present time?*
KENNAN: I don't think it's likely now, but I think it is going to happen eventually. I have noticed this about my own thoughts and diagnoses of the dynamics of the communist movement in the past. Very often the things that I and others who have lived in Russia have thought would happen, *have* indeed happened in the end. But they have come to pass more slowly than we had anticipated.

ALSOP: *Timing is the hardest thing to predict.*
KENNAN: Timing is, of course, the hardest thing to predict. But the operation of the great underlying principles of human society is not hard to predict. That is what the Soviet leaders will have to face up to, soon or late. I don't

mean for one moment to raise foolish expectations of an easy, automatic solution of the world problem. Until the Soviet Union changes very drastically, we must face and make the necessary effort to deal with the harsh military and political realities of the Soviet Union as it exists today. But we Americans must also learn to base our calculations and hope on the long-term realities of human nature and political behavior, not on the short-term ones. Confidence in these realities and the courage and patience to let them do their work are the things we need.

A Conversation with George Kennan

Melvin J. Lasky / 1960

From *Encounters*, March 1960.

LASKY: *There has been much recent discussion of the possibility of a slow change in the development of Soviet aims and goals towards something approaching more Western ideals and perhaps even Western methods. I wonder whether in your own professional field— diplomatic history—your experiences also lead you to that conclusion. Are Soviet historians working towards an ideal of greater truth in historical writing? What have their reactions been to your own two formidable volumes in the field of Russian history?*

KENNAN: One certainly could not say any such thing about official Soviet historiography. In recent years the "ideological section" of the Central Committee in Moscow appears to have been in the hands of people who hold the most violent prejudices of the Stalin era. These are people who consider the fund of historical knowledge not something which we study with a view to trying to determine what is true and what is not true, what really happened and what didn't happen, but rather as a sort of a great tremendous jack-pot, out of which you select whatever fact you need at the moment to bolster up a propaganda thesis. I must say that in all the record of modern tendentiousness, I have never seen anything as extreme as the recent official Russian historiography dealing with anything that concerns the Soviet Union itself. When I read this material, I can only conclude either that these people (and the Communist Party in Russia) are utterly unable to take any realistic account of the nature of Soviet power and of its experiences in the past; or else they know very well what the facts have been, and are terribly frightened that other people should learn of them. They make an extraordinary effort—an effort that sometimes seems almost to border on abnormality—to distort the past

17

and to build up the image of a mistreated, innocent Soviet government which never did anything wrong, never made a mistake, and which found, among its neighbours and the other powers of this earth, only régimes of the most villainous and diabolical intentions.

LASKY: *But could it not be that such methods are beginning to engender some new type of conflict somewhere in Soviet intellectual or historical circles—a conflict between their ideal of truth (and what they might think of as "scientific objectivity") and this ruthless and fairly cynical approach to documents and facts?*

KENNAN: I am absolutely confident that such a conflict exists and that it is destined to grow. We are beginning to see Soviet historians at international congresses; we read their journals—they obviously wish us to do so—and they read ours; they wish to be considered as serious historians, and many of them are. All this is going to mean, it seems to me, an inevitable confrontation of Russian scholars with the actual factual evidence. I cannot see how it could be otherwise. History is, after all, both a form of literature and a form of science; but as a form of science it exerts, in the last analysis, its own discipline on those who occupy themselves with it, and particularly those who begin to do so while they are still young. I think that you cannot ask a person to constitute himself as an historian who will in a certain area pursue the truth and in another area pursue untruth. This is too unnatural an occupation. I am sure it will not work over the long run. Younger Soviet scholars are, after all, not told that they should be complete propagandists. They are told that there is a certain field here for legitimate research. They are not going to be able to resist the infectious and the disciplinary quality of the pursuit of truth itself.

LASKY: *But I wonder what happens at an international conference in a debate between a "bourgeois historian" (and I suppose that's what you are labelled) and a "scientific socialist historian," when you get on to the subject of a document, or a footnote, or an exact date? Can one actually convince them because of this vague professional allegiance to the truth? Will they concede that the truth is above classes? How much do they still think they can "get away with"?*

KENNAN: I think that the actually documented and proven fact is a thing which they are obliged to recognise. All their efforts to get away from it will normally be in the field of interpretation. The tendentious ones try to select the facts that suit their particular thesis. Sometimes they are a bit callous in this. They select material which they think will sound factual or perhaps, for all I know, they may believe to be factual. I do think, however, that there is a certain common ground of respect for the provable fact on the basis of which we can discuss and argue. Frustrating as it may seem, it is a process to which we ought to subject ourselves; we ought to go through with it, and patiently. Over the long run, I am sure it will have its effect.

LASKY: *Do you feel that in this field, as in many others, cultural exchange will have a reciprocal influence, or will it be all rather one-sided?*
KENNAN: Oh, no. I am sure it will have reciprocal influence in every respect—and neither all to their advantage, nor to ours. I think there are things we can learn from them. But of course, the Soviet government has a curious idea of cultural exchange. For them it should have very closely defined limits, and should take place only in brief episodes which do not permit of any prolonged acquaintance or contact between the people on both sides. This seems to me regrettable and unworthy. They are not really so weak that they have to worry if one of their scholars carries on a personal correspondence, or has personal acquaintanceships in the outside world.

LASKY: *I have followed, of course, the Soviet comments on your own books. Isn't it a rather depressing debate? Here is some particular event of 1917, or 1919, or 1921, and you approach it in the light of your own idea of what a fact is, and what a proper interpretation is. They approach the same fact, ignore it, or displace it with another self-created fact.*
KENNAN: One thing, for example, on which I was very much surprised to be criticised was the interpretation of Lenin's decree on peace, which was published on the day after the Revolution, and which called upon the warring powers to lay down their arms. Now this decree was written in such a way as seemed to me to appeal to people directly over the heads of governments; it was quite an inflammatory nature. It was coupled with a demand that colonies be instantly released, and other rather flamboyant propaganda to which the Allied governments at that moment of extremity could certainly not have been expected to accede. I therefore pictured this as, first and foremost, a political and propaganda move designed to gain the confidence of the working masses in the warring countries, but *not* a serious bid to the governments for peace. I thought this was self-evident. But it appears to have aroused particular irritation with the Soviet historians. They cling to the theory that it was a perfectly normal bid in good faith by the Russians for an end to the war. Which rather surprises me. I don't think their early historians would have said this. But it

suits the needs of the present peace campaign, and they think it more important, apparently, to distort the real meaning of Lenin's actions in the interests
of their present peace campaign than to bring out the historical truth of the
early years of their régime. This seems to me quite extraordinary, really. I'm
sure that Lenin himself, were he alive to-day, would write in contemptuous
repudiation of all this. He would say, "Of course, we were revolutionaries, and
of course what we were working for was the world revolution. We were not
pacifists for the sake of pacifism."

LASKY: *But isn't this really a hang-over from the Stalinist era? Then there was such a
pathological sense of insecurity that they couldn't even adopt their normal Marxist method of
saying, "Look, things have changed. The situation at that time was thus and so. The situation
today is somewhat different. No contradiction at all!"*

KENNAN: Yes, that's quite true. There is a curious sort of a duality to-day in
the personality of the Soviet government. One sees that certain phases of
Soviet life are controlled and shaped by persons who have quite a lot of confidence in the new Russia, and find unnecessary these devices of the Stalin
age. But certain other forms of Soviet intellectual life, including the writing of
history, still seem to be, so far as the Party itself is concerned, under the
influence of people of whom that cannot be said, and who cling to all the
timidity and all the narrowness. Still, I would like to say this: if one looks at
the work of many of the younger Soviet historians, one sees that they have
been obliged for disciplinary reasons, and in order to be able to publish their
work at all, to cast it in the terms of some of these stereotyped concepts of
present Party doctrine. But if one looks at the substance of their articles, usu-
ally in the middle instead of the beginning or the end, one sees that they have
done some very serious and very competent and very useful research on various problems. And I think that, in itself, is a symptom that a bolder, a more
confident, a more worthy approach to the whole exercise of history is gradually coming to the Soviet historical fraternity.

LASKY: *Wouldn't you make a distinction here between the natural and the social sciences?
Objectivity in the laboratory has certain practical advantages, and it must have been a fairly
objective Soviet science which resulted in Sputnik and Lunik. But objectivity in the social
sciences surely has completely different kinds of consequences. They may want the practical
results of truth and logic and objectivity when they issue in technological power. But will
they ever want results which lead to a kind of intellectual facility and flexibility, to a certain*

tolerance, to a certain ability to see two sides of the question, to a certain scepticism—in other words, to all the worst virtues of "bourgeois liberalism"?

KENNAN: Well, they may not want it, but they are going to find that there is no other way forward except through the freedom of the mind. I am convinced of this, and I think that the entire younger generation in Russia feels this instinctively, and would be terribly, terribly reluctant to go the other way at this point in history.

LASKY: *If, then, this development goes further, and barring unforeseen set-backs and crises, do you foresee a cultural and intellectual situation, where, when a book like Boris Pasternak's comes on to the desks of the Soviet Publishing House, they could publish it and distribute it and review it and discuss it without feeling that the very bases of their society were being undermined?*

KENNAN: I think we are almost on the verge of that situation to-day. We may not even be far from the publication of Pasternak's novel in Russia. It would not have been so shocking for them to have done this at the start—nothing would have happened—the régime wouldn't have fallen. . . . It would merely have meant that the literature available to Russian people, which is already a rich literature and very much preoccupied with moral values, would have been further enriched by one more great novel, dealing with very much the same problems that Tolstoy and Dostoievsky and others, have dealt with. I suspect that they must have been very close to the publication of it. Again, it is only a rather shabby timidity, and one which seems to me quite unworthy of a country as great as this and as strong as this, which prevented them from doing it.

LASKY: *Was it essentially, then, only a bureaucratic, short-sighted top-level decision?*

KENNAN: I think so, one that they will live to regret from their own standards. I think they would have had far less trouble had they permitted the publication of this book; it would have been a sign of strength on their part and would have been taken as such by the younger people. After all, Mr. Khrushchev, I am sure, doesn't feel that they have anything to be ashamed of; he feels their record is one that can stand the scrutiny of daylight. Why not permit one honest and sensitive novel out of the early period of the Civil War to be published? This novel gave a picture, it is true, of the Civil War as a period of great confusion. Well, everyone in Russia knows that that's what it was! This was not an anti-Soviet novel; the people on the Left were not portrayed as fools or villains. I cannot understand this fear of having it said that life is what everybody knows it is.

LASKY: *I should like to shift the scene, for the next series of questions, from the Soviet world to the Western world, where surely there isn't a fear of any single book of this kind, where every year possibly not literary masterpieces like Pasternak's* Zhivago *but in the field of criticism and belles-lettres, a whole shelf-full of books are published which criticise, expose, and almost annihilate the very social-political foundations of Western society. Would you say that this is an unqualified source of strength? You have often dwelt on the "negative side" of American culture. One sees much with one's eyes, of course; but the major sources of information and persuasion are the big books of sociologists, economists, and political scientists. We look to a man like Galbraith to tell us what is wrong with our economic mores, we look to a man like Riesman to tell us where our psychological and social blockages occur. I have the feeling that we in the West all too easily say, "Of course, these books are written in criticism—therefore ours is a healthy society." Isn't that a bit like saying that because there are ten brilliant surgeons on hand to analyse a case of cancer, therefore the case of cancer isn't really as bad as it originally was? Can a balance be struck between our developing society and the critical intelligence that is being brought to bear on its problems?*
KENNAN: Well, I think you have come depressingly close to it with this analogy of the ten good doctors. I must say that I think these books have been extremely valuable, but I can't tell you what "beneficial effect" they have had in our society. I have been rather disappointed in our own American literature. We have had a whole series of novels which gave a bitterly critical picture of society, but so many of these books appear to me to reflect in their cynicism and in their hopelessness precisely the same evils against which they were written.

LASKY: *So many do seem so cheap in style and vulgar in intention. Think of how many have been written or the very same commercial motives which are condemned in their leading characters.*
KENNAN: Yes, exactly! But I would not say the same of the earlier "angry" period of the American novel—the time of Sinclair Lewis, Sherwood Anderson, John Dos Passos, Steinbeck, Thomas Wolfe, Eugene O'Neill. This was a more genuine critical literature with higher standards. Here was a real and deep search for the positive and for beauty, and not just the commercialisation of the negative.

LASKY: *Or could it be, George, that just as in certain historic epochs some of the best talents of the age went into painting, and in others into music; possibly this older American generation could express the conflict between conscience and society in the form of plays and novels, and our best contemporaries find themselves in social science, sociology, economics, criticism?*

KENNAN: It's perfectly possible, and undoubtedly, obviously I suppose, true. One sees this when one looks at the history of art and literature. To me these changes are very mysterious. I always wish that I knew why they occurred—why we should have had, for example, in the aftermath of World War I, so magnificent a flowering of literature in the United States—poetry and drama and the novel—as we actually did in the 20's, in that absolutely crazy, cock-eyed epoch, where the superficial values of society have never been less impressive. Nevertheless, underneath the surface we had those very remarkable people, whereas now we have them, quite as you say, in the other field of the social sciences.

LASKY: *Perhaps, then, if we are not exactly helping to heal the cancerous sores in our own society, we are doing something for the social or political hygiene of the rest of the Western world? In England and in Germany, throughout all of Western Europe, enlightened opinion seems to be turning to American social scientists. Could it be that we are in a way forerunners in both the disease and the diagnosis?*

KENNAN: Actually, of course, something very important is being done for American society in all this critical turmoil. The analogy you offer is faulty, because one cannot regard American society as hopelessly diseased. Every bit of self-scrutiny in a democratic society is healthy, and as our society is going to go on, for better or for worse, barring some catastrophe of the atom, it is certainly bound to be influenced by honest and penetrating self-criticism. And not only that. Somehow we Americans have made ourselves guilty over the course of the decades of great arrogance. Not the sort of ostentatious and cruel arrogance that has been exhibited by certain classes in Europe in the past, but a sort of childish arrogance about the virtues of our own society. It has not been a particularly nice trait. It has offended a great many people in the outside world. I think the spectacle of Americans actually looking at themselves, candidly and unsparingly, trying or the first time to get away from the romanticism of the 19th century, from the excitement and the provincialism of the whole frontier experience, taking account of themselves as a mature people—this is very inspiring.

LASKY: *But there has not only been this "childishness" or childish naïveté about American virtues. Surely over the last half-century, Henry James and after, Americans have also a naïve, possibly childishly naïve idea of their own vices. As if they were peculiarly American vices. The tale is familiar: there is no darkness in America; there are no châteaux; there is no tradition; American streets are rectangular and with no mis-shapen shadows where the spirit could dwell. And this was felt to be so because America was a new country and Europe was the vaunted scene of culture and humanist values. Now, we are all beginning to see a bit more clearly. We all share the problems of a commercial, industrial mass-society. We are all innocents, all decadents, all capitalists, all socialists, all bewildered angries. Suddenly we realise that maybe we're all in the same boat, or to go back to the old image—all on the same surgical table. Or are there some virtues and vices which are common to the West, and some virtues and vices which are peculiar to American civilisation?*

KENNAN: Our troubles are in part the troubles of the West, though not always with the same degree of intensity. In other respects, they are rather unique with ourselves. Specifically American, and not so relevant to Western Europe, is the enormous factor of wastefulness—the absolutely absurd wastefulness of American society. I am thinking of the relative thoughtlessness with which this society exhausts its natural resources, in deference to the dictatorship of commercial considerations; also the over-production, as Galbraith pointed out, of all goods which can be commercially sold, and the under-production of social services through the public authority.

LASKY: *Private wealth and public squalor.*

KENNAN: Yes, "private wealth and public squalor." I have also in mind the real damage that we have done to ourselves by the uncritical admission into our lives of the results of new technology. Of that, the automobile is exhibit No. 1. I think a growing number of Americans are persuaded that we have done untold damage to our society by permitting this sudden revolution in transportation from rails to the automobile. These two media of transportation have a precisely different disciplinary effect in the social sense—the railway, which was capable of accepting and disgorging its loads at fixed points, created the great railway metropolis of the 19th century, with all its unity, all its cultural excitement, all the things that made the great railway metropolises of that time what they were: London, Berlin, Chicago. The automobile has exactly the opposite effect. It is incapable of accepting or disgorging any great load of human bodies at any one place. It must fragmentise and explode that which has been united; and we have now succeeded in a land which prides itself on its local community, its local governmental arrangements, the "old New England town meeting," and so forth—we have succeeded in disintegrating the American community to an absolutely appalling degree: creating a complete chasm between the life and work, between the cultural centre and the place where influential people live, between real political power on the one hand and real economic and social power on the other. In every way we have fragmentised the elements of community at home. And we have had nothing very much to put in the place of those we have destroyed. When you see the depressing state of our great cities to-day, something which is far worse than the general aspect of our lives outside them, you realise the truth of this. Now this was only one gadget—the internal combustion engine—which we, without thinking, permitted to carry out this important revolution in our lives. There are certainly others—television is another very questionable one. I think it is high time we learned to ask ourselves how people ought to live. There are some parts of Europe where, it seems to me, some very tolerable solutions to these things have been found. In Switzerland, for example, the automobile and the railway, the bicycle and the human legs, exist very comfortably side by side. Elsewhere they are all at odds with each other and there is complete chaos. I am pleading here simply for a recognition of the subtlety and depth of the public problem involved—the problem involved for public authority in asking itself how is it desirable that people should live. What facilities should be given to them for life and work, how their lives should be arranged geographically, what opportunities ought to be offered to them for the use of their leisure. I don't want to tell people how to use their leisure; I do think they ought to have more opportunities than just the television set, or the local movie theatre. And isn't it up to us to create this?

LASKY: *This contemporary crisis would seem to be bound up with the problem of growth as a Western practice, possibly even as a Western fetish. Certainly to-day, as we see more and more, it has become something of an Eastern ideal. Doesn't the pattern embrace both underdeveloped countries as well as over-developed countries? The over-development is because of excessive growth—the under-development is because growth has not yet taken place.*
KENNAN: Well, anyone can see why the underdeveloped countries are terribly interested in this problem of economic growth. One can even understand why they are tempted to make a sort of fetish out of it. I personally think that they

are making a great mistake to wish to change their societies with the speed with which they actually seem to wish to do this. It is my own belief that if you change the lives of people so rapidly that the experience of the father, the wisdom of the father, become irrelevant to the needs of the son, you have done something very dangerous—you have broken the organic bond in the family, and you have created emotional trauma in the minds of young people. That is why I am a conservative. I think that the pace of change should always remain such that the parents have something to give to their children. I can remember very well the image of my own father, when he was a great deal older than I am to-day (he was born before our Civil War). In his old age, I, as a boy, could sense his depression and unhappiness at the realisation that this was an age he didn't understand; and that he had very little that was useful to tell me. But actually the modesty he showed in recognising this, was itself a great help to me. . . . I think that these leaders in the under-developed areas, who pursue economic growth with such concentrated passion, and are willing to sacrifice every other value to it, are mistaken. Nor do I, personally, see why one has to take the position that economic growth is essential to the health of our own Western society. I am constantly troubled by the things that I see written—and from very respectable economists—which reflect the view that our society can prosper and be what it should be only if it operates in a constant dynamic context—a quantitatively dynamic context.

LASKY: *Are you suggesting a qualitative turn in Western energy and dynamism, rather than the quantitative turn? I wonder whether your conservatism—or can one really speak of a kind of "revolutionary conservatism"?—can bear the burden of such a programme? What will be the equivalent of economic growth and economic dynamism in a country like the U.S.A. which for 150 years has been more or less exclusively devoted to that perspective? William James once used to worry about the moral equivalent of war. What is the moral equivalent of prosperity?*

KENNAN: Growth certainly shouldn't be an end in itself. It is supposed to serve some purpose. You see, what worries me about the prospect of unlimited, quantitative growth, is that this involves certain consequences that seem to me obviously undesirable. In the first place, if you are going to have unlimited productive growth, it implies also a steady growth in population and labour supply. And this really frightens me. While we are not entirely an "over-populated country," there are large portions of the United States that already have fully as many people in them as I would like to see them have. As you know, we expect soon to have a single semi-urban band all the way from the state of Maine down to Virginia, down the whole East coast—without really any open country or agriculture between. This is what my friend Jean Gottmann calls "Megalopolis," and a very bad use of land it is. It disrupts the community and the structure of local political life; it takes much too much land out of cultivation; it is ugly; it is a poor way for people to live. I don't want to see this population growth continue indefinitely in our country. Furthermore, economic growth—unlimited quantitative growth—means, it seems to me, a continued, rather reckless exhaustion of natural resources. I am afraid that if it continues in the spirit it is moving in at present, it also means a continued contamination of nature by man. This is a thing which worries me a great deal. There are not only the effects of atomic tests, the effects on the atmosphere; there is also the question of atomic waste, not just from the weapons development, but even from the peaceful uses of atomic energy. There is also the question of the use of highly poisonous insecticides in agriculture. People do this absolutely recklessly; they take aeroplanes, fly over a field in which they want to get rid of one given bug, poison they-don't-know'what, and upset the balance of nature very badly. There is the question of modern detergents, which are used in the homes in increasing numbers and are flowing out into the seas and doing certain things to the seas and to the vegetation life—things of which reputable scientists tell me we know only that the results are incalculable and irreversible, and we will not know for thirty or forty or fifty years what they really are. Now, this seems to me frivolous in the extreme, and defensible only if you say that the only thing that counts for us is these few remaining years of our own lives—that we are absolutely unconcerned as to the future, and for the lives of our children. There are other things I could mention. We know what the situation is with smog in so many crowded cities, making life extremely unpleasant and unhealthy. . . . It is all related to this spirit of expansion at all costs. I think it is high time we began to think about it. I'm all against it.

LASKY: *But it's at least a century since we were told that we've spent enough time "interpreting the world" and the time has come "to change it." Something must be done. But the surprising and paradoxical thing is that you are a conservative. I suppose you want not to "stop change" in some conservative or reactionary way of the last century, but rather to divert it.*

And not only divert it, but even revolutionise many institutions and many qualities of life. If I understand you correctly, you've come around to a feeling that public intervention is needed more than ever before—to a kind of new "dirigisme" in American and in Western life generally.

KENNAN: True. What I have in mind is not to stop change; it is not that at all. It is merely to govern its nature, because it has been taking a course which is completely uncontrolled, and in which the motivating impulses appear to have come from acquisitive private groups. These groups should not be permitted to have an absolute free hand. Actually, I think there is need for great change in our society. When I say we should stop the fetish of growth in the quantitative sense, I don't mean that there are not very very interesting and progressive and drastic things that need to be done. For one thing, our big cities need to be torn up and put together again. We have all become very keenly aware of the extremely unhealthy nature of the development of our cities over the past fifty years. The blocking of the central area; the moving of the people who have political and social influence out beyond the realms of the city; the sucking into the centre of the city of people at the very lowest level of education and income; the civic abandonment of these poor people by the more influential ones; the abandonment of the city administration to the people who make themselves leaders among these groups of extreme poverty—all this has given to our cities not only the depressing outward aspect that they have, but it has ruined them as cultural and political communities. There simply is no more element of community in them. Men cannot relate themselves in a proper way to the other men with whom they work and the men that live around them. There is no clear-cut definition of what is "community" in the neighbourhood of these great exploded cities of ours any more.

LASKY: *Is there a similar development in the small towns, or is this only true of New York, Philadelphia, Chicago, Los Angeles?*

KENNAN: What is happening in the small towns is also quite disturbing. I've seen it in my own village in Pennsylvania. The village used to have a political and communal life. People really lived there; their children went to school there; they went to church there; they did their shopping there; they worked there. To-day this is all changed. The village has become a row of houses along a highway, twenty-four minutes by automobile from the big industrial town of York. How many miles it is, is not important. Time has become important, not distance. These people are related to the industrial town of York, only by time, not by distance. And they are no longer neighbours of each other. There are some that work in the village, but a great many others don't— nor do they go to church there, nor do the young people do their courting there. The village is only a sort of a row of dormitories where they happen to sleep; it doesn't even maintain a policeman any more. They say: it costs money; and after all we're all just a lot of houses on a highway; and most of the things that happen here happen on the highway, and let the state police come in and settle it. Well, you see here the disintegration and corruption of the very roots of local government by this extreme mobility and dispersal which we permitted to come into the community. The village used to have a railway—the railway doesn't exist any more. It has no bus connection with any other place. Nobody can live in this village unless he has an automobile to get in and out.

LASKY: *This is, of course, to a far lesser extent, as we've already conceded, happening elsewhere. Isn't it happening in the subtopian developments of England? Certainly the British are very much concerned about it, although they haven't reached the point of disenchantment with highways—they're just on the verge of being enchanted with the idea of having their first hundred-mile stretch.*
KENNAN: One hundred miles?

LASKY: *They haven't built more than that. In fact, they say that the Romans built more during their years in England than the Anglo-Saxons built in the last ten centuries. Their enchantment is just beginning. The Germans have built their highways, and all their big cities, Frankfurt, Munich, Hamburg, are absolutely choked with traffic. There isn't a conceivable mathematical way of getting the traffic in and out of most of those urban labyrinths. And the smaller towns are also beginning to take on this character, as formidable prospering factories come in and set up their machinery on the outskirts. Where will the cultural, the intellectual, the moral resources come from—not only in America but in the West—in order to get a new vision of what we want to do? Is it "sociology" that's going to revivify us? Will it be some political leader who is going to come and give us a concept of a New Deal? How do you foresee the turn of events?*
KENNAN: Perhaps it will be not just one political leader, but a number of political leaders, as the understanding of these contemporary evils spreads. I think that new people are going to begin to come into political life who will see that things have to be done. Who will be doing the thinking? I have been

very much impressed with "the city planners": they have had their noses rubbed in these problems. The most interesting people I know to talk to about American life to-day, are some of these men who are working in the field of city planning.

LASKY: *Is this all a kind of pragmatic outburst, or are there books, ideas, memories of the past, which play a role? Is it a "Jeffersonian" ideal? Are there American philosophers or writers who have had a formative influence in shaping your notions and ideas and criticisms?* KENNAN: I suppose Lewis Mumford was the first—his book on *The Culture of Cities.* There is one illustration in his book, which I have never forgotten. It is an old picture, or rather an etching, of a procession in France at the end of the Middle Ages, and under it, as I recall it, there was a caption which ran something like this: "You will notice that there are no spectators. Everyone in town was in the procession, because everyone in town had some relation to the public life of the place." And this is what we have lost. . . . It will take a long time, but you see what we are working out is a science of the relationship of different functions of life to each other, geographically and otherwise. How far shall a man go to shop and to send his children to school? Is commuting, the dragging back and forth every day of a half-million human bodies over distances of fifteen to fifty miles from New York, is that a good thing to have happening? Should people live near their work? Should there be a factory district in a town, composed exclusively of factories and another district composed exclusively of residences? It's these sorts of questions which people are beginning to ask themselves, and they cut very deeply. They have this significance—that whereas the Marxists saw only the exploitation of man by man as a possible evil in the industrial revolution, people now see much more the urbanisation of society itself and the things that the machine does to man as the real trouble. And I cannot help but think of the tremendous insight that lies buried in one of Chekhov's stories. I believe it was called *A Case in Practice.* It was the story of a young country doctor who went over to the factory compound to treat a neurotic daughter of the factory owner. He found an unhappy wealthy household, actually dominated by a German governess. He had to stay there overnight and he observed these people. In the evening, after dinner, he sat down on the front steps and looked across at the buildings of the factory compound, thinking what an absurdity this was. Here, he thought to himself, were two thousand people who worked like slaves all day, as though in a dream, and only woke up on Saturday nights in the pub, and all of this merely in order that some cotton cloths could be sold cheaply on some Eastern market. The only beneficiary of this—obviously the only person that was made in any way happy by it was the German governess. . . .

LASKY: *Why the German governess?*
KENNAN: She was the only person who seemed to be doing well. And he arrived at the conclusion that all of this—the workers and their misery and the owners and their plight—was a kind of monstrous "misunderstanding." Think what a much more charitable interpretation that was than the interpretation of Marx. And he was absolutely correct—it is a huge misunderstanding—the misunderstanding of hasty and thoughtless industrialism in which both the entrepreneurs and the workers were all embraced, and which we are just now beginning to disentangle, and in a much more profound and much more charitable way, I think, than Marx tried to disentangle it.

LASKY: *I wonder whether we couldn't take the two subject-matters that we've been talking about and put them for a moment in a common focus. On the one hand, we have this Soviet Russian society, or rather this Soviet Communist world, going through certain late forms of the industrial revolution. It began fifty or sixty years ago, but is now bursting forth in all of its power, full of restless, dynamic energy, devoted in an almost American way to reaching out and exploiting natural resources, to expanding frontiers. You have been arguing over the years that this will somehow, possibly, become another kind of régime, another kind of a society—something "Beyond Communism." On the other side, we have American society, which has gotten to something like the last stages of its dynamic restlessness. It has achieved unparallelled material triumphs, and now is groping for a new or different kind of society— something, perhaps, "Beyond Capitalism." I wonder whether the international situation of the next five or ten or twenty years, will allow these basic forces moving in one place beyond (always in quotation marks) "Beyond Communism" and "Beyond Capitalism" to a new form of world order.*
KENNAN: You might think that what I am talking about would serve, in so far as it focuses attention on home, on internal problems, rather than external ones, to weaken resistance to international Communism. Wouldn't it make the nations of the West unmilitant, and thereby lead gradually to a disproportion of military strength? Well, there might be something in that, although not, I think, as much as people fear. In the first place, the impression that we make generally in the world is a part of our general political and military posture,

and it would certainly be improved to the extent that we address ourselves courageously and effectively to these problems. . . . I think that we can preserve what we need of a military posture.

LASKY: *But isn't the future danger more subtle? The West turns to its own social and economic problems, and possibly to new and daring solutions. Soviet society begins to go through this more flexible political and economic phase. American military and even political leadership begins to become increasingly meaningless. The battle of ideas and the struggle of loyalties takes on new forms. Won't more nations and peoples be looking more and more towards Moscow and Peking? Wouldn't our kind of society, despite our new urban planning and despite our new type of schools (or perhaps because of them) be a little strange to most of the ways of the world? Will we not be getting a gravitation of nations and peoples and public opinions towards the mechanical Soviet ways of progress, rather than our own?*

KENNAN: So far as Communism is concerned, it is a question of the true aims of Soviet power. Are the Soviets essentially a "Welfare State," that is, is their totalitarianism only a means to the rapid achievement of this end? Or has the totalitarianism become an end in itself, so that the ultimate aim is merely, as Raymond Aron has been arguing, "to bring about total tyranny in the name of abundance and liberation"? I doubt whether we can usefully pose this question so sharply, or invite so clean and tidy an answer. Russia is a country of contradictions. The history of Soviet power is one long record of the confusion of ends and means.

LASKY: *Would you then subscribe to the general view that the Soviet era is basically a continuation of the previous trends—under Tsarism—towards a modern industrial society?*

KENNAN: When the Russian Revolution occurred, Russia already was, and had been for some three or four decades, in a process of quite rapid evolution away from the archaic political and social institutions of Tsardom, in the direction of a modern liberal state. The development of a firm judicial system was far advanced; a beginning had been made towards local self-government; public opinion was becoming a force to be reckoned with. I have no reason to doubt that this represented the natural and underlying trend of Russian society in this country. It is a movement occurring somewhat later in time than, but otherwise not dissimilar from, comparable movement in Western countries.

LASKY: *1917 represents, then, more continuity than change?*

KENNAN: I would say that the Revolution in many ways did interrupt the long-

term trend of Russian society; but I do believe that this trend still represents
the direction in which, over the long run, Russia must move. I know you will
raise the question of Lenin. Yet despite Lenin's intolerant temperament and
the doctrinaire authoritarianism with which he governed his own party, there
can, I think be no question of the fundamental idealism of his purpose at the
time of the revolution. It was certainly with reluctance and with heaviness of
heart that he was obliged to concede, initially, the necessity of the terror.

LASKY: *But isn't terror the inevitable outcome of any attempt to put a Utopian vision into
practice by the use of political authority?*
KENNAN: I would agree. But I doubt that Lenin himself was aware of this. The
Bolshevik movement was betrayed into terrorism and brutality by the strange
sequence of events which carried it suddenly to power; revolution in a single
country, with minimal popular support and a tiny proletariat. Now instruments
of coercion once created have a tendency to find their own natural master.
With Stalin brutality was made into an end in itself.

LASKY: *Do you see in the theory and practice of his successors a fundamental break with his
methods and ideals?*
KENNAN: For Stalin these methods and ideals were the only way he knew to
protect his personal position and the integrity of his rule. Among a portion of
the officials of the Party and police, it came to be taken as the normal way of
government. To the people, at large, however, to the intelligentsia above all,
and even to a considerable portion of the Party, it was not only hateful but a
source of shame and humiliation. Among those who took this position, Khrushchev occupied a prominent place. But he was by no means alone, even
within the Praesidium. Most of his senior colleagues were prepared to concede
that a large portion of Stalin's methodology was unhealthy and undesirable,
though they often differed over the question as to how much of Stalinism
ought to be discarded and how much be retained.

LASKY: *What is your evaluation of how much has been discarded and how much retained?*
KENNAN: What we now see in the Soviet Union represents a compromise
among these differing views. The liberalisation has scarcely gone as far as
some would have liked to see it go. Nevertheless, it has gone so far as to
represent a highly significant departure from Stalinism and an essential alter-
ation of the nature of the régime. Can it move back? Of course it can; there

are no legal or constitutional barriers. But there is still a strong aversion in the older generation. And a younger generation is growing up which is habituated to a greater freedom and to greater expectation of personal comfort than they could have dreamed of some years ago. It would be extremely difficult, to-day to turn the clock back.

LASKY: *Yet, if we do not keep our eyes focused on Russia alone, I think you will agree that the pattern is confused. In certain outlying parts of the Soviet empire, notably in Eastern Germany, but also Czechoslovakia and Hungary, the movement away from Stalinism has not been nearly so marked. Is this greater totalitarianism a deliberate policy—or an accidental "national deviation" to the Right (as Poland is a "national deviation" to the Left)—or perhaps an involuntary or reluctant response to some "external necessities"?*

KENNAN: Of course there are still Stalinists in Moscow who find quite normal the manner in which Ulbricht's Germany is now governed. They would be happy to see the same principles applied elsewhere. But isn't it clear that this view has not always prevailed? Hence the significant variations within the satellite area itself. I believe the regions where Stalinist controls are most firmly maintained are those which are most neuralgic from the standpoint of the cold war. Poland repudiated of its own accord the excesses of Stalinist police terror—and persists stoutly in this repudiation—and Moscow has not seriously interfered.

LASKY: *Doesn't the Hungarian revolutionary experience indicate the point at which things might be considered to have gotten "out of hand"?*

KENNAN: The crucial limit of Russian patience, to judge from Hungary, relates less to the extent of internal liberalisation in a satellite country—provided, of course, the formal devotion to "socialist principle" is maintained—than to the degree of fidelity to the international security arrangements of which Moscow is the centre. Had the Nagy régime not moved in October 1956 to denounce the Warsaw Pact, in circumstances which gave the Russians no assurance whatsoever that Hungary, if permitted to take this step, would not end up by joining the Atlantic Pact instead, is it at all certain that the final Soviet intervention would ever have occurred?

LASKY: *You know, George, I disagree with that thesis sharply, and I think that the documents which I have included in my "White Book" on* The Hungarian Revolution *suggest a completely different reading of Soviet motives.*

KENNAN: That might be, but let's not lose ourselves in that argument now. My main point is that where strongly totalitarian features of government have endured in the Communist orbit, this has been for reasons having to do partly with the peculiarities of the local situation, or, in even greater part, with the pressures and necessities of the cold war. In neither case would the controlling fact appear to have been any such thing as a disposition on the part of the Soviet leadership to inflict these totalitarian devices for their own sakes.

LASKY: *Then the totalitarians, you would say, are slowly but surely on the way out?*
KENNAN: The picture, I reiterate, is not a simple one. On countless occasions when I have been asked which of two seemingly contradictory and incompatible realities is true in the Soviet Union, I have been obliged to say: both. The Stalinists are still there. They are people who, from habit, from fear, from limitation of vision, can think in no other terms than those of absolute domination. For them the Utopian end-product of socialism has become indistinguishable from a state of total political slavery. But these are only a portion of the leadership. They do not command the confidence of the oncoming generation. From the long-term—

LASKY: *And short-term? . . .*
KENNAN: Yes, and short-time standpoints they would appear to be on the side of the waning, not the waxing trends of Russian life. In the main, the goals and trends of Russian Communism lie along the same path as those of Western liberal-industrialism.

LASKY: *This is what I was suggesting by my earlier question about the prospects of moving "beyond Communism" and "beyond Capitalism." What, then, divides the two worlds?*
KENNAN: What divides the two worlds, in my thinking, is not a difference in aim. What divides them is fear, timidity, the unsolved problem of western Europe, and the unhappy dynamics of a weapons-race so absorbing that both sides tend to forget the issue of its origin.

LASKY: *But even if we concede your pattern of evolution, even if we reject an "absolutely negative" approach to Soviet society, there still remains a profound gap between the two worlds on such basic matters as the one-party régime, the suppression of criticism, and the systematic cultivation of falsehood. Aren't these all features of Soviet power that contrast basically with what we have in the West?*
KENNAN: The differences are undeniable, but they are relative and not abso-

lute. The deliberate cultivation of falsehood, as we were saying earlier on the subject of Russian historiography, seems to me to be undergoing, as a governmental policy, a process of severe erosion. I cannot imagine that it can be long continued in the manner of the past. As for the one-party system: it must be contrasted, unfortunately, with precisely that segment in the political life of the West which is itself to-day most subject to question, most doubtful in point of adequacy to the needs of the time. I mean the system of political parties and parliamentary institutions. In the doctrinal sense we in America also have in certain respects a one-party system. For aren't the two parties ideologically indistinguishable? Don't their pronouncements form one integral body of banality and platitude? And whoever does not care to work within their common framework, isn't he also condemned, like the non-party person in Russia, to political passivity—to an internal emigration?

LASKY: *I am afraid you will be widely misunderstood on this point, especially if you seem to be denying the validity of relative distinctions.*
KENNAN: I would be the last to want to deny them. I find our system, for all its shortcomings, vastly preferable to that which confronts it on the Communist side—if only because it interposes no political barrier to the freedom of the mind. But from the standpoint of the underdeveloped peoples, seeking inspiration and example—and here I think you seemed to be agreeing with me when you raised the question of the next stage in the struggle of ideas and loyalties—this relativity is significant. It spares the necessity of hard-and-fast choices. It seems to me overwhelmingly likely that there are going to be in the future as many forms of government in this world as there are genuine national entities. No single pattern—as is already evident in the Communist orbit—need be, or will be, universally imposed, and this need not worry us. Admittedly, the personality of the full-blown totalitarian state is an international problem, in the long run intolerable to the security of neighbouring states and to the interests of world peace. But for the endless varieties and gradations of normal authoritarianism we in the West can afford to manifest a relaxed and even sympathetic tolerance.

LASKY: *How do you feel about the possible Western perspective of "beyond Capitalism"?*
KENNAN: Well, this relates to the ideological principles, explicit or implicit, by which Western society is to-day informed. We have already touched upon some aspects—the lack of purpose, the lack of an answer as to the uses of

leisure, and the shrinking field of politics itself in a satiated world. I can't help repeating that there seem to me to be certain effects of our modern industrial society which, if not corrected in good time, could well cancel out many of its advantages. And when I speak again of "over-population" I am not thinking just of the relation of population to food supply, but also of the spiritual effects of over-crowdedness. On this, in our earlier talks, I think we have been one: the lack of privacy, the pervasive urbanisation, the difficulty of contact and communion with nature.

LASKY: *Would you associate these evils with the specific form of an economic and political system?*
KENNAN: When I ponder these evils I think they point to two deficiencies in outlook. The first is the restriction of the consciousness of obligation to the needs of the present generation alone—the self-centredness that regards Nature as an instrument and the convenience of contemporary man as an end in itself, as though there were no past and no future and as though man were not himself a part of Nature. I would plead for an end to this arrogant and hopeless attitude, and for the incorporation into the public philosophy of the West the recognition of the obligation to pass this planet on to future generations in a state no poorer, no less fair, no less capable of supporting the wonder of life, than that in which we found it. But secondly, I think these evils also have to do with the cult of production-for-production's sake. But we have already talked about the fetish of economic growth as an absolute good.

LASKY: *Here, too, I am afraid of misunderstanding—you will probably be marked down as a modern Luddite.*
KENNAN: Well, Raymond Aron has already been making light of this as the customary complaint of "conservatives and ex-Marxists." But some of us do sincerely believe that we see around us abundant evidence of the wholly un-critical adoption into our lives of devices which are on balance of doubtful benefit to the human condition—and just because they appear to represent a saving of labour or a speeding-up of the processes of production or daily life. It is all on the assumption that whatever is efficient can only be good and useful. I find this assumption unwarranted, and this standard highly debatable. I would submit that no ideology of modern industrialism can be adequate which does not embrace a thorough-going scepticism about all technological innovation beyond what is necessary to satisfy basic material needs.

LASKY: *Beyond that is a dangerous "over-development," but how can it be checked?*
KENNAN: Only by a readiness to take all this under the strictest sort of public control. Let science, by all means, be free. But its application to human life must be the object of man's sharpest distrust, and of the most severe social discipline. All of this points, again, to more *"dirigisme,"* not less, in Western society. I am sorry about this. To my mind, it is unfortunate. But I see no escape from it.

LASKY: *The necessity could be avoided, I suppose, if one were to renounce altogether—one occasionally hears this in Asia—the fruits of scientific and technical progress, and by retiring to a more primitive level of technology.*
KENNAN: This, let me emphasise, is not what I am advocating. The question is not whether public policy is to shape the lives of individuals. The question is whether the state is to acknowledge the responsibility for that shaping of the individual life which is already occurring by the processes which it tolerates or directs.

LASKY: *George, I wonder if in conclusion we could go back to the point of departure, namely your own work as an historian. You're finishing a third volume—will you remain as an historian in the field of American-Soviet relations, working with documents, or will you go on and address yourself to another historiographical task, or some other field in the Institute of Advanced Study? If you will just tell us a little bit about your own personal . . .*
KENNAN: Yes, but I don't know yet what I am going to do. It will be three or four years before I can really hope to finish my third volume; then I am inclined to doubt that I ought to go on with this sort of history. What I have done may have had certain value, but I am not really a very learned man as a historian, and have not read as widely and deeply as other people have who entered on this profession at the age of 25 instead of at the age of 50, as I did. I would rather, really, throw myself into work that was more closely connected with such things as literature and the aesthetic side of life, for which I think perhaps, particularly in the later years of my life, I have greater instinctive understanding.

Our Foreign Policy Is Paralyzed

Robert J. Moskin / 1963

From *Look*, 19 November 1963.

"Congress and the American people are so divided that American leadership is indecisive. It is high time we clarified our ideas as a nation and a government as to what we want in our contest with the Soviet Union and the rest of the Communist world: whether we want these countries to change, to capitulate to our desires, or whether we want war. People who hold all these three points of view have influence in Washington."

This warning comes from George F. Kennan, longtime expert on communism, former U.S. ambassador to the Soviet Union and to Yugoslavia, and a prime architect of the Marshall Plan. It is a rare event when a top-rank diplomat like Kennan, who has served twenty-nine years in the Foreign Service, breaks loose from The Establishment and speaks out on America's foreign-policy failings.

Kennan, fifty-nine, has fought for his convictions against Democrats and Republicans alike. He opposed Democratic Secretary of State Dean Acheson's German policy and was fired by Republican Secretary of State John Foster Dulles for disagreeing with his talk of the "liberation" of Easter Europe. Now, Kennan has resigned as President Kennedy's ambassador to Communist Yugoslavia because, he feels, the Congress and Washington bureaucracy had him hog-tied and have crippled American foreign policy.

After a lifetime in diplomacy, he was sent to the Soviet Union as soon as we recognized its existence in 1933; this tall, lean, imposing man sits now in his still-book-bare office at the Institute for Advanced Study in Princeton,

N.J., clasps and unclasps his hands, jumps up and paces the small room, peers out the window—as he struggles to say precisely what the American people should know about the state of their nation abroad.

In essence, he holds: We are fumbling because we have not made up our minds what kind of world we want, or what our role in the world should be. The Administration is zeroed in on political victory at home, enmeshed in bureaucratic red tape and buffeted by political cyclones that roar in from many directions. It sacrifices thought-out policies to pressures often inspired by "the powerful influence of the American Right Wing." Kennan fears that unless we nail down what we want our foreign policy to be, we will plummet to the ground in wing-clipped futility, or plunge into the flames of war.

"If we can't devise solutions better than this, we should ask ourselves whether we belong in the big leagues," Kennan warns. Indecisiveness at the top leads to a sterility of ideas and a failure to act. As a result, he argues, our foreign policy is paralyzed. A politician, whether in the White House or the Congress, who voices new ideas or acts with firmness in foreign affairs, must always protect his political life against extremists who talk loudly, but carry a very small stick of responsibility.

Kennan sees three forces paralyzing our foreign policy. The first is the Congress, in which a few powerful men—such as some leaders of the House Ways and Means Committee—tie up foreign policy. Some have strong notions about what the Government should be doing; others fear attacks from the extremists; some speak for special interests or jealously hug their prerogatives as holders of the nation's purse strings. There is no reason to believe, Kennan says, that their views represent American opinion more accurately than the President's.

The second force is the deadening hand of government bureaucracy. As an ambassador, Kennan found "the great difficulty was to get opinion and authority out of Washington, especially when it cost money."

The bureaucracy cannot react to changes fast enough. "Other countries find they are protected by our own financial procedures," he says. "The ponderousness of our government institutions works against our best interest."

The third force Kennan sees crippling our foreign policy is the self-interest of our allies. "The coalition is incapable of agreeing on any negotiated solutions except unconditional capitulation and the satisfaction of the maximum demands of each of our allies. It is easier for a coalition to agree to ask for everything but the kitchen sink, rather than take a real negotiating position.

"This worries me because there is not going to be any capitulation. Our adversaries are not that weak. If we cannot find any negotiating position, the Cold War will continue, and the dangers will not decrease."

The Russians may not accept our proposals, "but unless you dangle something before them, you put no pressure on their decision making."

Kennan sees no New Frontier in foreign affairs. "The Kennedy Administration is not by any means a free agent in foreign policy. I can see important changes in military policy. But in foreign policy, the Administration has had little latitude of action.

"Supposing these strictures did not exist and the Congress were more receptive? I believe we could usefully rethink our position on the problems of Germany and Central Europe. The same applies to the complex of problems surrounding Communist China, Taiwan and the Japanese peace treaty. We ought to review carefully our attitude toward Gen. Charles de Gaulle and see whether, under his concepts, France could not assume more of the burden of leadership in Western Europe and protection of Western Europe against Communist pressures. There ought to be searching reexamination and clarification of our policy toward Eastern Europe. The same applies to the various neutralist countries in Asia, Africa and Europe.

"Finally, there must be a real debate and clarification of our views on the problems of nuclear weapons. It seems dangerous to me that we should have to continue to stagger along with unresolved differences such as we have just witnessed in the debate on the test-ban treaty."

To illustrate how such forces paralyze out foreign policy, Kennan explains why he resigned from the State Department: "I had no difficulty with the Administration, but the actions which the Congress designed to tie the Administration's hands in our economic relations with Yugoslavia—and in a way that would deny the Yugoslavs normal commercial treatment—largely paralyzed my effectiveness there. If I had greater support on the Congressional side, and felt there were important possibilities for accomplishment, my decision might have been different."

Although the U.S. had millions of dollars in the bank in Yugoslavia, Kennan spent months getting Congressional approval even to repair the Embassy fence. "The jealous and narrow ways in which these matters are handled have to be changed."

Last July 26, an earthquake destroyed the Yugoslav city of Skopje, killing and injuring thousands. He has bitter memories: "The Congressional strictures were so severe that we didn't know how we could help. The only thing I could do was give blood. No Congressional committee could stop me from doing that."

Last year, the Congress directed the President to stop, as soon as practicable, normal most-favored-nation trade with any country dominated or controlled by communism. "The Yugoslavs aren't even asking [for] aid." Kennan says. They stopped taking military assistance from the U.S. in 1957. "They just want normal commercial treatment, and the Congress won't give it to them. That's very bad.

"I don't like to serve an Administration that has been told by Congress it can't aid a country if it wishes to. I feel very strongly it is foolish to deny normal commercial intercourse to a country facing important choices between East and West. . . . I don't favor any gifts to Yugoslavia, but I think it unfortunate that we should leave the long-term financing of Yugoslavia's industrial development entirely to Russia."

Kennan found some congressmen sympathetic toward his views on trade with Yugoslavia. They told him, "What you say is true, but I don't want to go back to my district having helped a Communist regime." Kennan charges: "This resulted in a position that gave aid and comfort to an enemy. They were interested in keeping themselves out of trouble."

He believes that much of the pressure on such congressmen comes from the Right Wing. "People are terribly sensitive to the charge that they are not sufficiently anti-Communist. The Right Wing has had an influence—it silences its opponents and makes everyone desirous of not being criticized from this quarter. A great part of the country stands silent on this. By far the greatest part of the American press is intimated."

He concludes: "There are tremendous issues that ought to be thoroughly debated and talked out and resolved in such a way as we can have a clear, vigorous and consistent policy in all these fields. These issues should not be allowed to smolder and paralyze national action."

Kennan sets forth four basic questions that Americans must answer for themselves:

Do we want to destroy, or negotiate with, Communist nations? At the heart of our international confusion is the question of "whether we are determined to destroy all these Communist regimes and inevitably have war, or are we determined to take advantage of such elements of moderation as may appear in the behavior of some of them, with a view of strengthening the chances of world peace?"

Kennan states bluntly where he stands: "People who expect the capitulation of Communist power are talking about something so unrealistic that they really want war." He calls their view "highly irresponsible."

Some Americans, in Kennan's view, see totalitarianism as a straight-jacket into which people get backed permanently. Others recognize it as "one illness of the human spirit from which societies recover."

He contrasts Khrushchev's regime which Stalin's: "I don't think it is more friendly toward us than Stalin's, but is probably ready to go farther in the direction of accommodation with us on questions of disarmament than was Stalin. The moderation of the internal terror and the greater liberality internally make it easier for us to deal with."

Looking beyond the Khrushchev era, Kennan says, "The demand of Russian youth for knowledge about the outside world and for freedom of expression has reached a dimension such that no Russian regime will be able to frustrate it entirely."

Do we want political or military solutions for the Cold War? Kennan has long felt that our thinking about the Cold War has been dominated by "over-militarization." We too often believe, if we have military superiority, the Communists must meet our demands.

To Kennan, Europe is a political problem. This judgment led to his break with Secretary of State Acheson. Kennan advocated a withdrawal from the center of Europe. Acheson, he recalls, took "violent exception" to this idea of "disengagement" and blasted it as "a timid and defeatist policy of retreat" and "the new isolationism." Kennan still disagrees with Acheson's claim that if the great powers were to withdraw, all Europe would go down on its knees. He points to the Austrians: "They didn't go down on their knees. The Finns have done nothing of the sort."

As a result of this, "overmilitarized" thinking, Kennan believes we have mishandled postwar Germany. "Ever since 1950, when Mr. Acheson proceeded to the rearming of West Germany, I've had misgivings about it. This has been a serious handicap on our policy in Eastern Europe. All of them fear Germany and don't want to see Germany rearmed. This is one fear that is shared by the people and the regimes of Eastern Europe.

"It wouldn't have hurt the Germans to have had at least 20 years of demilitarization."

Kennan would like to see a unified but neutralized Germany possessing only weapons for defense. "None of this can be changed overnight. The West Germans are members of NATO, and we have to respect that status. I'm talking about a disposition to change some of these arrangements if, and only if, the Russians will make some compensation—only as part of a deal."

As Kennan sees it, two factors block the reunification of Germany: "We are inhibited by feeling the need of a strong U.S. military force in West Germany, even if the Russians withdraw in East Germany. They are inhibited by the disgraceful weakness of the Ulbricht regime." We should press the Russians to replace it. "They realize they are holding up a regime which has no popular support. I believe someday Russia will have to abandon East Germany and let it rejoin Germany."

Disengagement in Europe has not become American policy, but Kennan's ideas about the "containment" of Soviet power have greatly influenced our approach to the Soviet Union. They also triggered his being fired from the Foreign Service in 1953 by Secretary of State Dulles, or, as Emmet John Hughes has written, "discourteously dismissed."

Kennan is convinced that Dulles's talk of rescuing Eastern Europe damaged the United States. "Mr. Dulles liked to talk about liberation of Eastern Europe, but did nothing about it. I prefer not to talk about it. Mr, Dulles talked a line designed to appease the Right Wing critics of our policy, and followed the same policy as in the past. I have felt we should not talk in a way we did not intend to act." The effect of Dulles's words was "to tighten the apron strings of the satellite governments to the Soviet Union." Kennan warns that we still have not made up our minds "whether we want Eastern Europe to evolve in our direction, or whether we want to overthrow these governments."

On what basis should we give aid to other nations? Kennan argues that economic and military aid is no checkrein to keep teetering nations from dropping into the pit of communism. "I am personally skeptical about foreign aid, especially when it is given as a condition of not going Communist. We should help those who say, 'We are going to survive whether you help us or not'—like

Finland. When a country says, 'If you don't help us, we will go under,' we should get off the trolley."

Jumping off the trolley can be a tricky maneuver, as the U.S. Government was reminded recently when it reexamined its choices of action in South Vietnam. Kennan wants to take a tough look at regimes like Ngo Dinh Diem's. "We should appraise them—neither take too tragic a view of them nor underrate them. When you have regimes of this sort, they are awful fast to take advantage of your willingness to help them. You always have to be ready to get out."

If we find people unable to help themselves, but still consider their area vital, Kennan adds, "then we have to be ready to take over entirely, and be ready to face the charges of colonialism—and we have to be very leery, very cautious of that."

He thinks getting out of South Vietnam is a possibility to be considered: "Let's not overdramatize the results. Let's look at it realistically. It will be bad, but not as bad as we sometimes think. Politically, I regard the Chinese as much more deeply committed against us than the Russians." However, he adds, "the Chinese Communists are not yet a substantial naval or air power. It does not bear the same military implications as Russia taking over. On the contrary, there is such a thing as overextension."

How should we react to the Soviet-Chinese split? "The Soviet-Chinese conflict represents one of those turns of events in the face of which a great nation has no excuse not to think through its policies toward the Communist world."

Kennan sees little hope of establishing relations with the Chinese Communists now. He thinks they are "much too violent, wild, emotional." Yet, he contends, "the day will come when they settle down and we can have talks with them. We should be prepared to talk to the devil himself, if he controls enough of the world to make it worth our while."

He regards recognition of Communist China as "nothing more than the opening of a channel of communication—not a reward or approval." But, he says, "I am not sure they are even prepared to treat an American representative properly. I think we might have de facto recognition, keep a charge there as the British do, if they will treat him properly."

Of Communist China entering the UN, he says, "I don't think they would be a very constructive member of the UN—any more than the Russians have been. But if a majority of members wanted them in, we would put ourselves on a misleading position by holding out against it. This too is not some kind of reward."

How can the United States rid itself of the jellylike indecision that paralyzes our foreign policy? Kennan points to three alternatives.

First, if we are not going to act as a powerful and responsible leader of the free world, we had better get out of the arena. Kennan does not advocate isolationism; but he feels that the present chaos is worse than isolation. Americans are not used to compromises and dealings with a formidable adversary in peacetime. We need, he says, either to strengthen the Executive's freedom to act in foreign affairs or quit. "We lived for more than 100 years on principles of withdrawal from the mainstream, and maybe this should be done again."

His second alternative is to modify our political system. "Our form of government is not well suited to making decisions." The reason for this, he says, is that "power is too much fragmented in Washington, including the Congress, the armed forces, the FBI—all the people who decide our national actions."

Kennan suggests that we move closer to a parliamentary system. We could regard the off-year Congressional elections between Presidential elections as a vote of confidence on the Administration's policies. If a President felt the vote showed that he was not supported in the country, he could be free to call a presidential election immediately. To those who fear this idea, Kennan emphasizes that it would have to be made by amending the Constitution. "There's nothing treasonable about that."

Kennan's third alternative is to mount a public debate over foreign policy so that the American people can understand the issues, make up their minds about them and reach a consensus. Out of such a debate, Kennan hopes, can come an American viewpoint—a body of instruction to the President and a body of support. "You must have a crystallization of dominant public opinion. Our international position calls for this kind of clarification—calls urgently for it—in such a way that perhaps it is the last call. It can't come too soon."

Oral History Interview with George F. Kennan

Louis Fischer / 1965

MR. FISCHER: *March 23, 1965. This is an interview with Mr. George F. Kennan who was United States Ambassador to Moscow and, during the Kennedy Administration, to Belgrade. We are seated in Mr. Kennan's office in the Institute for Advanced Study where he is Professor and permanent member of the faculty of Historical Studies. I am Louis Fischer, author of books on the Soviet Union, on India, etc. With us in the office is Mr. Charles Morrissey, Chief of the Oral History Project of the John F. Kennedy Library, and, also, Mr. Kennan's fifteen-year-old son, Christopher. Mr. Kennan and I are old friends, and it would be stilted and formal to address one another as Mr. or Professor, so it will just be "George" and "Louis." George, what acquaintance did you have with John F. Kennedy prior to his election as President?*

MR. KENNAN: Well, I had seen him and heard from him several times. So far as I can recall, the first time I met him was at a party in Washington in the early 1950s: I think, actually, around 1953, at the time that I was leaving the Foreign Service for the first time.* Then, I once spoke from the same platform with him at Brandeis University at a later period in the '50s. I can't remember just when it was, but probably around 1958. It was an afternoon ceremony devoted to foreign students in this country; he and I were both speakers. Of course, I met him, and I met Mrs. Kennedy, again on that occasion.

MR. FISCHER: *How did he speak? Do you recall?*

MR. KENNAN: I thought—reasonably well, but not greatly effectively because

---

*Mr. Kennan retired twice from the Foreign Service: once in 1953, and again after his service in Yugoslavia.

he was then deeply immersed in political life. He gave a great many such speeches. This was, I think, one written for him, and he just read it off. It was all right; it was suitable. But one didn't have the impression that it was a statement to which he himself had given a great deal of thought and which came out of his heart, so to speak.

MR. FISCHER: *What impression did he make on you as a person?*
MR. KENNAN: On those occasions merely a pleasant one. I was impressed with his youthfulness—he looked like a sort of an overgrown student in those days. I was impressed with Mrs. Kennedy's beauty. But these were very casual meetings. I can't remember whether he was a Senator on both of those occasions or not. Perhaps he was.

MR. MORRISSEY: *In 1953 he would have been just beginning.*
MR. KENNAN: Of course, I was amazed to see anyone looking so young and so modest in the Senatorial position.

MR. FISCHER: *Did you ever have any correspondence with John F. Kennedy before his candidacy or election as President?*
MR. KENNAN: Yes, I had several exchanges of communications with him. On February 13, 1958, when I was living and teaching at Oxford in England, I was very surprised and pleased to receive from him a letter about the Reith Lectures which I had recently delivered in England on the BBC. Those lectures are, of course, the annual BBC lecture series, that is the main series of their "Third Program." The ones that I delivered in the autumn of 1957 received, I think, a particularly large amount of attention. The BBC told me that all six of them had had listening audiences greater than any lecture previously given on the BBC except for the initial Reith lecture, the first one given by Bertrand Russell when they were started, which had about the same. They were rebroadcast in this country and in Canada, and they were actually heard by millions of people. They were completed in the middle of December, and it was in February that I received this letter from the then Senator Kennedy.

MR. FISCHER: *Yes. Would you please read it?*
MR. KENNAN: Yes. It was addressed to me in England—correctly to my home address there in Oxford. Wherever he got it, I don't know.

"Dear Mr. Kennan: Having had an opportunity to read in full your Reith Lectures, I should like to convey to you my respect for their brilliance and stimulation and to commend you for the service you have performed by delivering them. I have studied the lectures with care and find that their contents have become twisted and misrepresented in many of the criticisms made of them. Needless to say, there is nothing in these lectures or in your career of public service which justifies the personal criticisms that have been made. I myself take a differing attitude toward several of the matters which you raised in these lectures—especially as regards the underdeveloped world—but it is most satisfying that there is at least one member of the "opposition" who is not only performing his critical duty but also providing a carefully formulated, comprehensive and brilliantly written set of alternative proposals and perspectives. You have directed our attention to the right questions and in a manner that allows us to test rigorously our current assumptions. I am very pleased to learn that these lectures will soon be published in book form, almost simultaneously with the appearance of the second volume of your magistral study of U.S.-Soviet relations after World War I. With kind regards and every good wish for your stay in Oxford, Sincerely yours, John F. Kennedy."

MR. FISCHER: *That's remarkable, and I'm sure you were very pleased. George, could you give us in a paragraph or so the thesis, or theses, of your Reith Lectures, so that there would be a background for this letter?*
MR. KENNAN: The main thesis was a plea for reexamination by our policy makers of the questions of disengagement in Europe and of disarmament. But also there was one lecture, and it is this to which he particularly refers there, which dealt with the underdeveloped world, and which carried forward—I think for the first time from myself publicly—the thesis that we ought to be prepared to let some of these countries go Communist when they try to blackmail us with threats along those lines rather than overloading them with aid.

MR. FISCHER: *It's to this that he took exception?*
MR. KENNAN: I think it is to this that he took exception.

MR. FISCHER: *Where had he read these?*
MR. KENNAN: They were very widely published in excerpts and other ways for this kind of thing.

MR. FISCHER: *He must have read them in a British publication.*

MR. KENNAN: I think he read them in the *Listener* because later he wrote me about other things of mine that appeared in the *Listener*. I think he saw the *Listener*, which is the organ of the BBC. They were all published in full in the *Listener*. But they were also republished in many ways elsewhere.

MR. FISCHER: *There was great charity in that letter.*
MR. KENNAN: There certainly was. I was, of course, particularly moved that he should know about my scholarly work. Very few people knew where that stood at that moment.

MR. FISCHER: *I wonder how he did know.*
MR. KENNAN: I don't know.

MR. MORRISSEY: *Could you tell us the date of that letter?*
MR. KENNAN: That letter was written to me on February 13, 1958.

MR. FISCHER: *How was he aware of the attacks? He says personal attacks.*
MR. KENNAN: I think he had in mind, particularly, the attacks levied against me by Dean Acheson and by a group of so-called German "experts," who were close to Acheson and close to the Bonn (West German) government, who attacked me very bitterly. There were something like fourteen of them. These attacks were, indeed, to some extent personal, and I was deeply upset about them because Mr. Acheson, in particular, took occasion to reproach me publicly for recommendations I had made to him as his subordinate in government several years earlier—recommendations which he had not acceded to, which he had rejected, and which I had never taken to the public as an issue, you see. This seemed to me to be improper because I felt that any man who serves in an advisory capacity in government has a right to give his honest advice to his superior. But the superior must not reproach him with it later, publicly, because it was his duty to give him his honest judgment.

MR. FISCHER: *Then the letter from Senator Kennedy was certainly balm for you.*
MR. KENNAN: It certainly was. . . .

MR. FISCHER: *And I suppose it was so intended.*
MR. KENNAN: Yes, I'm sure it was. I'm sure that he didn't feel that this was the right way to respond to the lectures—by personal attacks.

Would you like me to go on with the other communications I had from him then in that period?

MR. FISCHER: *Yes, I was about to ask.*

MR. KENNAN: Nearly a year later on January 21, 1959, I had another letter from him concerning two more things that I had written that had come to his attention. One of these was an article entitled "Disengagement Revisited" which had appeared in the January 1959 issue of *Foreign Affairs*. This was really a reply to Mr. Acheson and to the other critics of the Reith Lectures. The other article to which he referred was a piece entitled "America's Administrative Response to Its World Problems." This was a contribution I had made at a conference at MIT, and it dealt with the problem of Washington bureaucracy, with the growth of administrative staffs in Washington. He had read this, too. It was these two that were mentioned in his letter. Now, since his letter refers to the content of these, it might be advisable for me to mention one or two of the things stated in the article about "Disengagement Revisited." It was a reexamination of the assumptions of our policy in Germany, especially the assumptions with relation to the Soviet Union. I'll read the letter. This was written on stationery of the Senate January 21, 1959, addressed to me here at the Institute.

"Dear Mr. Kennan: I understand there is a chance that you may be in Washington during the next weeks, perhaps to testify before the Foreign Relations Committee. At all events, I am most anxious to have the opportunity of talking with you when you are next here. If you would let me know just a little beforehand by letter or telephone, I would be most happy to have you for lunch or dinner—or even breakfast if that suits you best. During the holidays I had the opportunity to read both your article in the current issue of *Foreign Affairs* and your earlier piece on "America's Administrative Response to Its World Problems." Both of these articles raise issues which I would very much like to discuss with you. I think that you have made it unmistakably clear in the *Foreign Affairs* article what we must negotiate about if we hold talks with the Russians and I think you have disposed of the extreme rigidity of Mr. Acheson's position with great effectiveness and without the kind of *ad hominem* irrelevancies in which Mr. Acheson unfortunately indulged last year. . . ."

MR. FISCHER: *Very interesting. Now, what happened, George? Did you see him?*

MR. KENNAN: I did arrange to have lunch with him when I went to Washington to testify, shortly after that, at some hearings which were conducted by Senator Humphrey. But, actually, as I recall it, his schedule was cluttered up that day, and the best I was able to do was call on him in his office in the afternoon, briefly. I can remember that only as a sort of a courtesy call in which he was pretty harried. He had some labor union problem on his mind, and I didn't detain him long because I could see what sort of things he was into.

Now, that was in January 1959. A year later, in January 1960, again I had a note from him. This time, a handwritten note undated except for "Monday" and written in Jamaica, where he was vacationing. This was, of course, within a few months of his [subsequent] nomination and election as President.

MR. FISCHER: *Before, yes.*

MR. KENNAN: Yes. While I will be glad to turn this note over to you, it is, as you see, a handwritten item. As far as I can read it this is what it says: "I had the opportunity belatedly today of reading your talk reprinted in the October issue of the *Listener*. It impressed me, as does everything you say, with its dispassionate good sense. I was especially interested in your thoughts on our considering not merely limitations in testing but the abrogation of the weapon itself. I wonder if we could expect to check the sweep south of the Chinese with their endless armies with conventional forces? In any case, we shall all be discussing this two or three years after the moment of opportunity has passed. I hope to see you when you are in Washington after the first of the year. Good wishes for you for Christmas and peace on earth. Sincerely, John Kennedy."

MR. FISCHER: *That's very warm and prescient, I think.*

MR. KENNAN: Yes, and this letter is of particular interest because of its reference to testing and to the question of abolishing the atomic weapon. I thought, for that reason, I might read here one or two of the key passages of the article which he had read and to which he refers, to which he was responding. I had pointed out that, whereas the Russians had manifested at all times since 1945 a readiness in principle and even an eagerness to agree on the total abolition and outlawing of atomic weapons, we in the West had taken an ambiguous position on this. And I go ahead here in citing what was said in the article: "We appear, in particular, to have committed ourselves extensively in our military planning to what is called the 'principle of first use.' This position is intelligible only on the hypothesis that we consider ourselves to be outclassed in the field of conventional weapons, that we are looking to the

atomic ones to redress the balance, that we could, therefore, view an abolition
of atomic weapons only as an unacceptable deterioration in our strategic situation, and that we would be disinclined, accordingly, to agree to any such
abolition unless it were accompanied by a wide measure of disarmament in
conventional weapons as well." That's one passage. I then polemized later in
the article with this position that we couldn't defend ourselves with conventional weapons and said: "So far as our weakness in conventional weapons is
concerned, let us be frank with ourselves. This is a matter of convenience and
of political will. The resources of the NATO group are in no way inferior to
those of the Soviet Union when it comes to the ingredients of conventional
military power. Whether we develop or fail to develop these resources is a
matter of our own political choice. I am wholly unwilling to believe that we
could not compete militarily in an atomless world. Can one seriously suppose
that, had atomic weapons never been invented, the western nations would not
have found means to assure their own security in this postwar period? Plainly,
the abolition of the atomic weapons would free considerable financial and
technical resources for the improvement of the conventional ones, and, if this
improvement also involved more disciplined mobilization and utilization of
manpower, this, too, would be cheap at the price compared to the dangers we
now face." And, then, finally, I polemized in this article against the cultivation
of the weapons of mass destruction because they threatened, as I said, "the
very intactness of the natural environment in which civilization is to proceed
if it is to proceed at all." I would like to quote the passage that follows, because
of the fact that he wrote me this note. "I must say that to do anything that has
this effect [and that is to threaten the intactness of our natural environment]
seems to me simply wrong. Wrong in the good, old-fashioned meaning of the
term. It involves an egocentricity on our part that has no foundation either in
religious faith or in political philosophy. It accords poorly with the view we
like to take of ourselves as people whose lives are founded on a system of
spiritual and ethical values. We of this generation did not create the civilization of which we are a part and, only too obviously, it is not we who are
destined to complete it. We are not the owners of the planet we inhabit; we
are only its custodians. There are limitations on the extent to which we should
be permitted to devastate or pollute it. Our own safety and convenience is not
the ultimate of what is at stake in the judgment of these problems. People did
not struggle and sacrifice and endure over the course of several thousand years

to produce this civilization merely in order to make it possible for us, the contemporaries of 1959, to make an end to it or to place it in jeopardy at our pleasure for the sake of our own personal safety. If we are to regard ourselves as the heir to a tradition and as the bearers of a faith, or even a culture, then our deepest obligation must be realized as relating not to ourselves alone but to that which we represent, not to the present alone but to the past and to the future." So much for the excerpts. This was, of course, another speech given on the BBC and reprinted in the *Listener.* I cite these passages because it does seem to me important that he should have written to me concentrating on this question of the atomic weapon. It is important from the standpoint of the fact that during his subsequent administration he did move both to the limitation of testing and, also, to the strengthening of conventional weapons as a means of getting away from an exclusive dependence on the atomic ones. Both of these things begin to appear in here.

MR. FISCHER: *George, did you have any contact with John F. Kennedy between the time of his election and the time he took office?*
MR. KENNAN: Louis, before I go on to that, I ought, perhaps, to tell you about one more communication. Two more, actually, that I had with him. The first was that I, of course, acknowledged this letter he had written to me about the *Listener* article, and I had a reply very shortly after that to the effect that he had read a further article of mine which was the one which appeared in *Foreign Affairs* in which I polemized with Khrushchev on the subject of coexistence.

MR. FISCHER: *Oh yes, I remember that—a very good article.*
MR. KENNAN: You remember Khrushchev had had an article in *Foreign Affairs* defining the Soviet idea of coexistence? I was asked to write a reply to it and did. This he had read, and this is a very brief. . . . I thought I might just read it into the record because then we have a complete record of what he wrote me in those years. January 26, 1960, written from the Senate. "Dear Mr. Kennan: Thank you very much for your kind personal letter elaborating on the article in the *Listener.* Meanwhile I have also received a copy of your article in the current issue of Foreign Affairs. I think that your article is most effective and masterfully written. The tone and content of this article could hardly be better. I hope that there may be an opportunity of chatting with you again on one of your future visits to Washington." Now, that brought us up to the election. Shortly after the [nomination], but before he took office, I, taking

advantage of what appeared to me to be his interest in my views, sat down and wrote him on August 17, 1960, a long letter putting before him my views about some of our basic problems of foreign policy, particularly with regard to the Soviet Union, and making a number of points which I thought he might like to bear in mind in the final stages of his campaign. That is a long letter, and I will not read it all into the record. I give you a copy of it, but I might read the summary paragraph of it, to let you know what sort of thing I had said to him in this letter. "Let me then summarize. We may, by January, be faced with an extremely disturbing if not calamitous situation. It will in any case be an unfavorable one and in urgent need of improvement. Such a situation could be brought under control only if we could regain the initiative. To do this, a new administration should move quickly and boldly in the initial stages of its incumbency, before it becomes enmeshed in the procedural tangles of Washington and before it is itself placed on the defensive by the movement of events. The needed curtailment of our world commitments gives opportunities for initiative, but it should be balanced by a strengthening of our defense posture, particularly in the conventional weapons. The main target of our diplomacy should be to heighten the divisive tendencies within the Soviet bloc. The best means to do this lies in the improvement of our relations with Moscow. An effort along these lines is essential to any sound policy, but this should not lead us into any new involvements concerning summit meetings, nor should it be assumed that it necessitates the extensive negotiation of formal agreements." I might explain that I had pressed him here, particularly, to take advantage of the opportunities for private communication with the Soviet government. I had taken a position against trying to solve our problems with the Russians in general by concluding formal agreements which would require Congressional approval in our country and would get the suspicions of the Russians up. (The Russians always become suspicious when one gets legalistic about language with them.) I had urged him here to try to seek an improvement of our relations with the Soviet Union by reciprocal concessions—that we do something that eases their position; they, then, do something that eases ours, and each one is a pledge of good faith for the next one. In order to be able to do that, I recommend—and this is important because I'll return to this later when we discuss my own work in Belgrade—I had recommended that we make maximum use of the possibilities of private, fully private, discussion with the Soviet government. I said, "These things are difficult, but they are not, I reiterate, impossible. [That is, private discussions, with them.] And, if private discussions of this sort happen to provide the only favorable possibilities, as they did actually in the liquidation of the Berlin blockade and the Korean War, then we cannot afford to spurn them. Let us remember that a series of conciliatory moves on the part of our government, which would be quite unsuitable if they were to be made without corresponding action on the other side, might well be acceptable if they were to be matched and geared in with a similar series of concessions on the other side. Neither party would have to assume any obligation to the other in this respect, but there is no reason in principle why one should not keep in touch, informally, with people on the Soviet side with a view to making such a process of settling issues by unilateral actions as painless and productive as possible." He wrote me on October 30, only a week before the election, on stationery of the Senate from Washington: "Dear Mr. Kennan: I just want to let you know that I profited greatly from the long letter which you were so kind to send me some weeks back, and I am especially conscious of some of the suggestions it made as we reach these last days of the campaign. I am very much in accord with the main thrust of your argument and with most of your particular recommendations. I hope, win or lose, that there may be an opportunity of seeing you after the election is over. May I thank you for your generous willingness to support me publicly in this campaign. With every good wish, Sincerely yours, John F. Kennedy." That completes, Louis, the record of the exchanges that I had with him prior to his election.

MR. FISCHER: *What happened between his election and his inauguration? Did you see him or correspond with him*
MR. KENNAN: Yes. On January 3, 1961, I had a phone call from his office inviting me to come to New York on the tenth of January, 1961, and to lunch with him. I accepted and went up there, but his schedule—these were, of course, the hectic days between his election and his assumption of office— turned out to be very heavily burdened that day. So he asked me, instead of lunching with him in New York, to get on his private plane, on which he was about to fly to Washington, to fly with him, and to have lunch on the plane. This I did. He came out and sat with me while I had lunch. (There were a number of other people on the plane.) We talked for a portion of the journey down to Washington. I kept a record of this conversation with him. It's the

only one of the several conversations that I had with him in that period and further, later on, during his Presidency, of which I have a personal record. I was at that time not in government so there was no question of classification, and I could write this all down for my own purposes. I will not read you the whole record because it's lengthy. I might, however, read certain passages which give some idea of what he was interested in. I quote—this memo, incidentally, is dated January 10, 1961: "He began by telling me of the many approaches made to him from the Soviet side, particularly through Menshikov, in recent weeks. [I might explain that Menshikov was then, I believe, the Soviet Ambassador in Washington.] He said that to put an end to the many indirect approaches, he had asked Bruce to talk to Menshikov and find our specifically what he had in mind."

MR. FISCHER: *That's our Ambassador, David Bruce.*
MR. KENNAN: Yes. "And he showed me the memo Bruce had written about this talk to which there was attached an unsigned and unletterheaded document in which Menshikov had set forth what purported to be his own personal thoughts. This document, which bore to my eye all the earmarks of having been drafted in Khrushchev's office but cleared with a wider circle of people, was considerably stiffer and more offensive than Menshikov's own remarks. Both documents stressed the urgency of negotiation and invited exchanges looking toward a summit meeting. Mr. Kennedy asked me what I thought of them, and what he ought to do about them." I don't know whether to go on with my own reply to this. It will be in the record if you want it, but this passage that I have just quoted shows the nature of his problems at that time.

MR. FISCHER: *I think it would be interesting to get the impression of the colloquy.*
MR. KENNAN: All right. "I explained that I thought there were two camps in the Kremlin, not neatly and clearly delimited but nevertheless importantly different, one of which did not care about relations with this country because it considered that we could be successfully disposed of despite ourselves and without need for any negotiations; the other of which was reluctant to burn the bridges. I thought Mr. Menshikov's statement, which specifically mentioned his being in touch with Khrushchev, Mikoyan, and Kozlov, indicated that he was speaking personally for this latter group. On the other hand the written document had probably had to be cleared with a wider circle and was, therefore, tougher in content. I said that I saw no reason why he should take

any official cognizance of the written document or give it any specific reply. As for Menshikov and his urgings, I said that in his position I would make no reply to Menshikov or to Khrushchev before taking office. These people had no right whatsoever to rush him in this way, and he was under no obligation of any sort to conduct any communication with foreign governments prior to his assumption of office. As for the subsequent period, I was inclined to think that it might be well to send a private and confidential message to Khrushchev saying, in effect, that if people on that side were serious in their desire to discuss with us any of the major outstanding differences between the two governments, including disarmament, there would be a positive and constructive response on our side. But when it came to suggestions for summit meetings, the burden of proof first of all would be on anyone who wanted such a meeting to demonstrate why these questions could not be better treated at lower and more normal levels. In any case, it was difficult to see how an American President could conceivably meet with people who were putting their signatures to the sort of anti-American propaganda which had recently been emanating from Moscow and Peking. I reiterated that I thought such a message ought to be drafted so as to bear publication in case the Russians spilled it or it leaked in any other way. However, I said, he ought not to take any step of this sort just on the basis of my advice. [Charles] Bohlen and Averell Harriman should also be consulted as well as [Llewellyn] Thompson— those were the other three men who had served as Ambassador in Moscow. And he should listen to their views both on the desirability of making such a communication and on the question of the channels by which it might best be sent. In this connection I told him at a later point in the conversation that I hoped he would insist on the right of privacy in the handling of the Soviet problem. I thought the outgoing administration had gone much too far in accepting the thesis that nothing should be done with the Russians which should not immediately be made known to the press. In my opinion privacy of communication with other governments was a right of his office and one of which he could not let himself be deprived without detriment to his possibilities for conducting policy successfully. He asked why I thought Khrushchev was so eager for a summit meeting. I said that I felt that his position had been weakened and explained why. This, I might interject here, I felt had been the consequence of the U-2 episode.

MR. FISCHER: *And the break-up of the summit meeting.*

[Portions omitted because of classification restrictions]

MR. KENNAN: . . . was a real sense of urgency in Moscow about achieving agreements on disarmament, and that this stemmed largely from concern over the "nth country" problem and particularly China. Khrushchev, I thought, still hoped that by the insertion of his own personality and the use of his powers of persuasion he could achieve such an agreement with the United States and recoup in this way his failing political fortunes.

Senator Kennedy said that he was giving thought to the problem of staff with relation to foreign policy. He wondered whether he should not have around him in the White House a small staff of people who worked just for him and did not represent other departments. He said that he did not want to be put in a position where he had only one or two people to whom he could turn for certain types of advice. He said that Rusk had already come to him about our possible intervention in Laos. He felt that this was too narrow a basis of advice for decisions of such gravity. He did not want to be in the position of Mr. Truman, who had, in effect, only one foreign policy advisor, namely Mr. Acheson, and was entirely dependent on what advice the latter gave. I said that it was and had been for long my emphatic view that the President should have staff of his own and should not be dependent merely on advice that came up through the various departments and agencies. I will not go ahead with all my views on that unless you think it necessary.

MR. FISCHER: *Did you find him a good listener?*
MR. KENNAN: Excellent always. He is the best listener I've ever seen in high position anywhere. I might say at this point that what impressed me most of all about Mr. Kennedy over the course of the years, as I saw him repeatedly, was the fact that he was able to resist the temptation, to which so many other great men have yielded, to sound off himself and be admired. He asked questions modestly, sensibly, and listened very patiently to what you had to say and did not try, then, to tell jokes, to be laughed at, or to utter sententious statements himself to be admired. This is a rare thing among men who have arisen to very exalted positions. I don't want to name other names, but I can think of some of the greatest with whom it was very hard, indeed, to have a conversation because they tended to monopolize it.

MR. FISCHER: *Did you sense at that time, on that airplane trip, that he was already the President of the United States?*

MR. KENNAN: Oh, yes. Very much so. He was feeling his way. He sincerely wanted advice—the broadest and best advice he could get, and I was well aware that my voice was only one of many that he was consulting. I fully approved of that by telling him that I felt that on certain of these subjects he ought to. . . .

MR. FISCHER: *George, did he make any suggestion to you about your personal participation?*

MR. KENNAN: Not yet.

MR. FISCHER: *Not on that trip?*

MR. KENNAN: No. I might read on a bit here because there are two or three other indications of what he had in mind. He told me of certain of his difficulties choosing people, and I don't think I need to repeat that; it mentions the people in question. We talked about who would be good for the policy planning staff and that sort of thing.

MR. FISCHER: *I'm not asking you for the names, but was he seeking advice? Was he asking for guidance?*

MR. KENNAN: Yes, he knew that I had been director of the policy planning staff, and he did want my views as to what sort of a person would be good to fill that position. We talked about foreign aid; I gave him my views on that, urged that we concentrate on India, said I thought we had wasted large amounts of the aid. We talked about the Foreign Service and the State Department. I told him I thought both were grotesquely overstaffed and gave him my views on that. On leaving him in Washington, I thanked him for his courtesy and assured him both of my enthusiasm for the way he was going about his tasks and of my readiness to be of service to him in any way that I could. At some point in the conversation, incidentally, he said that "he had made it a rule not to consider any diplomatic appointments prior to his assumption of office. In pursuance of this ruling he had resisted some very heavy pressures from the political side. He had done this for the sake of the career service, and he hoped the men in the service realized this and would repay him in loyalty and application accordingly. He then talked to me about the question of the ambassadorship in Moscow, whether he should make a change there— Thompson was there. I said that I thought it'd be an excellent thing if he could keep Thompson there at least for the immediate future, but I thought that he ought to be called home at an early date and consulted by the President about the problems of our relations with the Soviet Union."

MR. FISCHER: *There was no intimation tentatively about what he wanted you to do?*
MR. KENNAN: Not then but very shortly thereafter. This meeting on the plane was on the tenth of January. Very shortly thereafter, on January 23rd, when I was up at Yale University where I was teaching a weekly seminar, I just happened to walk into the office of the college at which I resided, and with which I was connected up there, to see whether there was any mail for me. I wasn't spending the morning there, in fact I was going along the street. But I thought, "I'll just walk into the college office and see if there's a letter for me." As I walked in there—it was the noon hour and the regular secretary was gone— there was an undergraduate who was tending the telephone in the office. He got up, and I could see that he was agitated. He had the telephone receiver in one hand, and he said, "Mr. Kennan, you came just at the right second. The President of the United States wants to talk to you." This was, indeed, Mr. Kennedy—President Kennedy. He had now been in office for what was it— three days. He asked me whether I would be prepared to serve as ambassador either in Poland or in Yugoslavia, and, if so, which I would prefer. I told him that I would be happy to serve, and I would give him an answer as to which I would prefer very shortly, if possible later in the day. So I did. I thought it over for the rest of the day and called him back in the evening and told him I would prefer to serve in Yugoslavia.

MR. FISCHER: *George, out of your knowledge of diplomatic procedure, is this the normal way of doing things? Of a President calling a private citizen and asking this sort of question?*
MR. KENNAN: I think it is. That is, he might, more normally, in more leisurely days have asked such a citizen to come to Washington to see him. But I could well understand he had a great deal to do in a short time. I thought it was a very courteous way. He could have done this through the Secretary of State. But this was the proper way because an ambassador is the personal representative of the President. Therefore, it is really proper, in my opinion, that the President should ask him to serve and almost important that this should come this way. I don't know whether this is always done this way or not.

MR. FISCHER: *Did he say anything else? How did he begin the conversation?*

MR. KENNAN: You know, I can't remember exactly, but I think he put it to me very bluntly. I think he simply said that "I would hope that you would consent to serve as ambassador for me, and I have two posts that I'm interested in your filling." So, from that time on I had agreed, of course, to serve. Then, very shortly after that, I was asked to come to Washington and to confer with him. I did this. The date named was February 11th. I went down there and met in his office with a group of people who included Vice President Lyndon Johnson, MacGeorge Bundy, and the other three men who had been ambassadors to the Soviet Union, Harriman, Thompson, and Bohlen. The purpose of this was simply to get our advice on problems of relations with the Soviet Union and the Communist bloc. I don't remember the conversation. I would have voiced sentiments similar to the ones that I expressed to him in the plane. The Vice President, as I recall it, said nothing and merely sat in. I had the impression he felt that he was just there to be briefed. The only thing that I remember about that is that, at the end of our conversation, Cuba came up and the question of a possible intervention in Cuba by these exiles. This was, of course, only two months before the Bay of Pigs episode. I can remember both Bohlen and myself telling him that "whatever you feel you have to do here, be sure that it is successful; because the worst thing is to undertake something of this sort and to undertake it unsuccessfully."

MR. FISCHER: *The best kind of advice. How long did that conversation last?*
MR. KENNAN: This was a Saturday morning, as I recall it, and it lasted most of the morning. I think from about nine-thirty or ten to twelve. It was a long session.

MR. FISCHER: *What do you feel he was after? Anything specific or . . .*
MR. KENNAN: He wanted to know how to tackle the main problem of diplomacy for him which was relations with the Soviet Union, to what extent he should credit the good will of the approaches that were being made on the other side, whether he should have a summit meeting, how he should go about this. He was very uncertain about all this.

MR. FISCHER: *Do you think he had made up his mind to go into a summit meeting and wanted your advice?*
MR. KENNAN: No, I do not think that he had made up his mind at that time. He was very troubled about this problem because, having been in Congress,

he was very sensitive to the strong anti-Communist feelings that were prevalent in a portion of the electorate and in a large portion of the Congress. He wanted to handle this problem, if he could, in such a way as to make progress in composing our differences with the Russians, but not to get himself attacked at home for being soft on Communism or anything of that sort.

MR. FISCHER: *On Cuba did you have an impression that he had already made up his mind to intervene?*
MR. KENNAN: No, but I had the impression that he was being pressed to authorize intervention or to wink at it. That is my recollection. I saw him incidentally, once more then before I left for my post. I paid a formal call on him on March 22nd, the day that I was sworn in as Ambassador. I cannot remember what we discussed. It would have been partly with relation to Yugoslavia, partly again, probably, the Soviet problem. He always sought my advice on problems of relations with Russia as well as on Yugoslavia.

MR. FISCHER: *George, how long did you serve at Belgrade?*
MR. KENNAN: I served there from the first days of May 1961 until about the last day of July 1963. In other words, I was actually at my post about two years and a quarter although my actual period of being formally ambassador was somewhat longer than that.

MR. FISCHER: *Would you now give us an account of your contacts with the President either in person or in writing during that period?*
MR. KENNAN: Yes. First of all, it was my understanding from what I was told by Mac Bundy and others that the President gave instructions that all of my major political telegrams and communications were to be sent over for his personal reading.

MR. FISCHER: *Sent over from the State Department?*
MR. KENNAN: From the State Department. I don't think that this was the case with very many ambassadors, but he did want to see—either he or Bundy or both—practically everything that I sent in. I think that one reason he did was that I tried to make these communications have a little more flavor and a little more interest and put a bit of humor in them and make them a bit peppery to get away from the dullness of normal official communications. He always enjoyed that. In addition to this, during this period that I served in Belgrade, I was called home to Washington five times. Four times for consultation on the

problems of my post and once to accompany the Yugoslav Foreign Minister, who was passing through Washington and who wanted to call on the President.

MR. FISCHER: *That was Koĉa Popovíc?*
MR. KENNAN: That was Koĉa Popovíc. The President thought that it would be advisable for me to be there. He wanted to consult with me before he received Popovíc and wanted me to escort Popovíc to see him. So I was called home five times in all, and on every one of these occasions I saw the President. I didn't have to take the initiative in asking to see him. He always knew I was coming home and asked to see me. He simply made known the time when he would see me. I don't have the records of our conversations on those occasions. I remember with particular distinctness the time that I took Popovíc to see him. I had already seen the President alone the day before and told him what I thought would be on Popovíc's mind, and what sort of line I thought he ought to take. Then I did, of course, accompany Popovíc and sit there with him during the interview. I was full of admiration for the way the President handled him.

MR. FISCHER: *Popovíc speaks good French. Did he speak French?*
MR. KENNAN: He spoke English.

MR. FISCHER: *He spoke English.*
MR. KENNAN: Yes. He doesn't like to, but he can. On this occasion he spoke English. The President received him in his upstairs sitting room, motioned him over to the sofa, sat down in his rocking chair, and began to question him. He couldn't have asked him a better question than the one he started with. It really made, I am sure, a deep impression on Popovíc because it was so different from the usual beginning of such a diplomatic conversation.

MR. FISCHER: *And what was that?*
MR. KENNAN: What the President said to him was substantially this: "Mr. Minister, you are a Marxist, and the Marxist doctrine has had certain clear ideas about how things were to develop in this world. When you look over the things that have happened in the years since the Russian Revolution, does it seem to you that the way the world is developing is the way that Marx envisaged it, or do you see any variations here or any divergencies from Marx's predictions?"

MR. FISCHER: *Wonderful question!*

MR. KENNAN: Yes. I don't think he got a very clear answer from Popović on this, but he asked it in such a humble and disarming way that Popović couldn't be annoyed with him because it was entirely respectful and apparently naive, you know.

MR. FISCHER: *But hardly naive.*

MR. KENNAN: It was hardly naive. But he did very well; he was courteous, hospitable, kindly, and relaxed with him, not at all stiff, showed himself to be in no hurry, was quite prepared to let him talk. He had, on this as on other occasions when he received foreign visitors, a sort of a boyish, crude but very impressive courtesy—instinctive courtesy—which seemed to me to be rather Lincolnesque. It was a sort of Lindberghian boyishness—like Lindbergh, you know. There was something very appealing about it. There were no elaborate fancy manners connected with it. It was very quiet, but all the more impressive for this reason. Everyone understood it and got it right away. They realized that this man had a certain old-fashioned gallantry about him, really, in everything that he did, and they responded to it. Popović did on this occasion and Tito later when I took him to see the President—very much so.

MR. FISCHER: *Was the President aiming at some goal in this conversation with Koĉa Popović?*

MR. KENNAN: No. I don't think that . . .

MR. FISCHER: *Either for his own education or in the way of achieving some kind of better relations with Yugoslavia?*

MR. KENNAN: Well, this came at a very unhappy moment, and the President knew that he had no backing in Congress for a constructive policy toward Yugoslavia. The result is that he rather avoided getting into questions of Yugoslav-American relations.

MR. FISCHER: *Did he ask Popović about the Soviet Union? I'm interested in knowing whether the Soviet Union was very much on his mind.*

MR. KENNAN: As I recall it, I think he did. I think on both of these occasions with Popović and later with Tito that he pressed them both to say what they thought of Soviet policy. Popović, of course, is a very intelligent man, very sharp, the ex-military commander of the Yugoslav forces in the Partisan War all the way through, and then who had been a military commander in Spain.

MR. FISCHER: *But, also, a poet.*
MR. KENNAN: Also a poet. Very sharp, a man who didn't suffer fools gladly.

MR. FISCHER: *That wouldn't have arisen on this occasion.*
MR. KENNAN: He had no opportunity to demonstrate that peculiarity in his character. Actually, I liked Popovíc and respected him. He was a very sensitive man and a bit bristly, but I never had any complaint against him.

MR. FISCHER: *I suppose you left with Popovíc.*
MR. KENNAN: I left that interview with Popovíc.

MR. FISCHER: *Yes, that's what I mean. Did Popovíc at that time, or at any other time, give you his impressions of Kennedy?*
MR. KENNAN: I can't recall that he did. I think he was reserved.

MR. FISCHER: *Would you go on with any subsequent contacts? Did the President respond to any of your reports or messages that you sent through the State Department?*
MR. KENNAN: Only through Bundy as I recall it. I suppose I ought to go on and tell about the difficulties I encountered at this post. Of course, it was normally my task there to try to improve the relations between our country and Yugoslavia. I thought it very important to do this for several reasons. First, because if we could achieve a mutually profitable and pleasant relation with Yugoslavia, it would help to fortify that country in its position of independence vis-à-vis the Soviet bloc. But not only would it fortify the Yugoslavs in this position, it would encourage other satellite countries to move in the same direction. This, I thought, was of the greatest importance in view of the Chinese-Soviet conflict. As you know, I was a person who had been concerned with the Soviet Union and with matters of world Communism for many, many years, so that this seemed to me a very serious question.

MR. FISCHER: *George, on your arrival in Belgrade as Ambassador what impression did you get of the feelings that the Yugoslav leaders, particularly Tito and Koĉa Popovíc and others, had towards Kennedy as President and towards you as his representative?*
MR. KENNAN: With regard to the President they were uncertain. They simply didn't know what they were up against. They wanted to see how he was going to conduct himself. They had encountered many difficulties, in their relations with the United States, at the hands of certain elements of the Catholic church hierarchy in this country, and I think this made them uncertain as to

what they could expect from Mr. Kennedy. You see, the Croatian exile element in the United States, being strongly Catholic, had been very prominent in stirring up trouble for them in Catholic circles here, and especially in the hierarchy in certain parts of the country, and they didn't quite know what they were getting into.

MR. FISCHER: *Because they thought that Kennedy might act as a Catholic?*
MR. KENNAN: Yes, and that he might then be responsive to the pressures from these Croatian émigré circles which they regarded, and with a great deal of justification, as thoroughly Nazi in their political views. In other words, as fascists.

MR. FISCHER: *Were the Yugoslav leaders conscious of the internal political situation in the United States—say the small majority by which Kennedy had been elected?*
MR. KENNAN: Yes, they were quite aware of that. They knew that, in general, his position had been a somewhat more liberal one than that of the previous administration.

MR. FISCHER: *How did they know that? Was that the speech on Algeria?*
MR. KENNAN: From his speeches and from his campaign statements. But on the other hand they realized that it hadn't been *much* more liberal, that the real issues had not come out in the campaign, and they were not certain as to which way the cat would jump. So that, so far as the President was concerned, it was a case of their waiting to see. I think Tito, in particular, was skeptical. Tito had been very deeply shocked by the U-2 episode; it had affected, very greatly, his confidence in American statesmanship, and it had to be proven to him that the new President was going to get away from this sort of thing. He tended to see our policy as dominated by the military and the CIA. Of course, the Bay of Pigs episode, happening just the day I left Washington to go to my new post, was not helpful. On the other hand toward myself, personally, the Yugoslavs were extremely cordial, and I think they were very pleased with my assignment there. I got this in many roundabout ways as I arrived. I think the reasons for this were these: They had been favorably impressed by the Reith Lectures and by the positions on East-West relations. I had, just as it happened, visited Yugoslavia the previous summer, in the summer of 1960, and had had an interview with Tito on that occasion. When I was named Ambassador, the Yugoslavs immediately formed the impression that I had come the

previous summer, as they said, "to case the joint," and nothing could cure them of this. But in any case they were pleased; they viewed me as a person who understood the Russian problem, who understood their position, and who was a man of peace. Furthermore, they considered me, rightly or wrongly, a distinguished person in the United States, and they were pleased that someone whose name they had heard before was being sent to Belgrade. They viewed this as a sign that President Kennedy did attach importance to the relations between the United States and Yugoslavia.

MR. FISCHER: *George, you of course, had a conversation with Tito when you presented your letters of credence.*
MR. KENNAN: I did.

MR. FISCHER: *You must have seen Edvard Kardelj and others. Did they ask about Kennedy? What were they interested in about Kennedy?*
MR. KENNAN: I cannot remember that they asked personally about Kennedy. I do not recall those conversations sufficiently well. They were interested, of course, in our policy, and they were very anxious to explain their own view of things. They believed in disarmament; they believed in disengagements; they wanted to see the military tensions reduced; they felt, as Tito always said to me, that we ought not to dramatize our differences with the Soviet Union; they thought that Khrushchev was, for all his angularities, a man of peace— that we didn't understand this, that we were better off with him than we were likely to be with anybody else.

MR. FISCHER: *Did they think that Kennedy did not understand this?*
MR. KENNAN: They didn't know yet but they felt that, in general, American statesmanship had been clumsy . . .

MR. FISCHER: *That is, in the previous administration.*
MR. KENNAN: . . . and over-militaristic in its handling of the whole Soviet problem, and they wanted to explain to us why they felt this. Also, of course, they had very strong feelings—and ones with which in very large part I could not agree—on our policies toward the underdeveloped areas, toward places like Vietnam and all that. They wanted to see us withdraw militarily every-where and leave the decision to local forces.

MR. FISCHER: *George, do you feel that you were successful in accomplishing the mission that President Kennedy had assigned to you?*

MR. KENNAN: Definitely not, if the mission be considered one of improving relations and establishing a sound relationship and good understanding between Yugoslavia and the United States. I felt my mission in this respect was a failure, and it was so marked a failure, really, that I felt personally discredited and obliged to leave the post after this period of two and a quarter years.

MR. FISCHER: *Were the difficulties from the Yugoslav side or from the American side or both?*
MR. KENNAN: There were difficulties from both sides. I might mention the Yugoslav ones first because they came generally first, chronologically. It was only shortly after I arrived there—only about four months after I arrived—that they had the Belgrade Conference. . . .

MR. FISCHER: *The Belgrade Conference of so-called non-aligned nations.*
MR. KENNAN: . . . In which the heads of state of some twenty-five so-called non-aligned nations assembled in Belgrade. On this occasion Tito made statements, both in his speeches, and, as I recall it, outside, which came as a shock to us, which seemed to be definitely unneutral, which seemed to be weighted on the Soviet side, which were a very serious jolt to our relations, which caused a formal protest on the part of our government in Belgrade.

MR. FISCHER: *Did you stimulate this?*
MR. KENNAN: I did not stimulate it, and it came as a particularly unpleasant surprise to me because I had been given the impression, prior to the conference, that what he would say at the conference would be quite agreeable to us. I have the feeling that something happened in the last two or three days before that conference began which changed all this and caused him to come down very strongly on the Soviet side. I think I know what that was. First of all at this particular time, Tito was very concerned to register, so far as he could, his solidarity with Khrushchev on world problems. This was for two main reasons. First, in the light of the Soviet-Chinese conflict. The full seriousness of this conflict had only recently become visible—outstandingly at a Communist conference which was held in Bucharest, as I recall it, in June 1960.

MR. FISCHER: *Yes, I remember.*
MR. KENNAN: This had made a deep impression on Tito, especially the fact that the Albanians had gone over to the support of the Chinese, and were being used by the Chinese as a weapon, made him feel that he had to support

Soviet influence in Eastern Europe to some extent and certainly Soviet influence in the world Communist movement generally against the Chinese. For this reason he did his best to emphasize the points where he was in agreement with Khrushchev. But, in addition to this, he realized that the Russians now wanted his support very badly, that in order to defend themselves against the Chinese attacks the Russians had to be able to argue that Yugoslavia, after all, was a good socialist country, that it was as strongly anti-imperialist as anyone else, that it had not abandoned its socialist principles . . .

MR. FISCHER: *As the Chinese were asserting.*

MR. KENNAN: . . . as the Chinese were asserting. And he wanted to give Khrushchev ammunition with which to prove before the world public and especially the world Communist public that Yugoslavia's position as an independent Communist nation was not detrimental to the world Communist cause, that Yugoslavia was a loyal and helpful member, in that respect, of the ideological family even though she occupied an independent political and military position. He felt that Khrushchev, too, needed help. I'm quite sure morally that he was appealed to just before the Belgrade Conference to give Khrushchev help because of Khrushchev's own personal position in Russia. The result was that he said these things at the Conference which came as such as jolt to us. Now, it is true, and I realized this more later as I served in Yugoslavia than I realized it at the time, that this was not anything new, that repeatedly over the course of the years Tito had rocked this boat by making statements which sounded very pro Soviet, and therefore, came as a jolt to the American representatives in Yugoslavia and to our public opinion. But this hit me particularly hard for certain reasons. You know, the Yugoslavs at that time often came to me and said: "Why did you react so sharply to the things that Tito said at the Belgrade Conference? These are only things we've been saying for years." I said: "Yes, but they have not been things that were said by your President in the presence of twenty-five other chiefs of state with seven or eight hundred foreign newspaper correspondents in attendance. When you say things like this on such an occasion, they go deeply, and you have to realize that we can't pass them off so lightly."

MR. FISCHER: *And they echo in Washington, yet.*

MR. KENNAN: They echo in Washington. Immediately after the Conference I received a large group of foreign correspondents at the Embassy. I talked to

them for about an hour, and I explained to them the reason why these statements were unacceptable to us. The Yugoslavs didn't like this at all. It took
me some time to live this down with them, but I felt that they had to be
advised of the full extent to which they were damaging their position abroad.
In any case, this did a lot of damage because these statements were picked up,
of course, by our press; they were played up and, as Tito would say, drama-
tized by the headline writers and so forth. They definitely did increase the
bad press that Yugoslavia had already had in this country.

MR. FISCHER: *Would you refer specifically to Tito's statement about the explosion of the
Soviet Union?*
MR. KENNAN: Yes. I think the thing that came as the greatest blow to us was
that just one day before the Conference opened . . .

MR. FISCHER: *Yes, September 1.*
MR. KENNAN: On the very day that it opened (it was September 1). . . . (it
was the day that he was greeting these arriving heads of state out at the air-
field), the Soviets announced the resumption of testing.

MR. FISCHER: *And of giant bombs.*
MR. KENNAN: Yes, nuclear testing. This was in violation of the existing understanding.

MR. FISCHER: *Tacit understanding.*
MR. KENNAN: Yes, tacit understanding. Had we done this, we would have been
lambasted endlessly in the Yugoslav press. As it is, when Tito came to speak
at the Belgrade Conference, there was inserted in between the lines in his
speech, or on a little separate slip of paper which was attached to the copies
of the speech given to us, a statement to the effect that he understood the
Soviet reasons for resuming testing. I am sure that this was the result of some
twisting of his arm that was done by the Soviet Ambassador on the eve of the
Conference. Of course, it looked all the worse because it looked as though
the Russians were in a position to make him say anything they wanted to. The
Soviet Ambassador had gone all the way out to the airport to see him that
day in the midst of these arrivals, and I'm sure that something was said. It must
have been a message from Khrushchev to the extent that "if I ever needed
your help, I need it now, and I want you to support me on this particular
position."

MR. FISCHER: *Did you talk to any of the chiefs of state at that Conference? Did you see Nehru or . . .?*

MR. KENNAN: I did see Nehru briefly, and he is the only chief of state, I think, that asked to see me there. Oh yes, I also had to speak, officially, with Sukarno because the Conference decided to send a joint appeal both to the United States and Russia. Sukarno was charged with transmitting that to us which he did through me. So he called me over to this hotel.

MR. FISCHER: *Did Nehru talk about Kennedy?*

MR. KENNAN: No, he didn't. Again, it turned out to be very hectic and unsatisfactory. We only had a few moments to speak, and I can't remember that there was any more said other than pleasantries and platitudes.

MR. FISCHER: *Did Sukarno assume that he was going to see President Kennedy?*

MR. KENNAN: Yes, Sukarno was there with an entourage of some sixty people with a great Pan-American jet plane which he had been hiring steadily for some months. He was about to take off for Washington to deliver this message.

MR. FISCHER: *And he wanted to see the President?*

MR. KENNAN: Yes. I can't remember in what connection I was called in, but it was in connection with this message, and I had to go over and accept the advance copy of it or something like that. But those were the only two heads of state I can recall seeing. However, I would emphasize this Belgrade Conference because it made my task much more difficult. I felt, in a way, that Tito had really let me down. Of course, I understood better after I had been there longer why he felt that, in such a situation, this was the best move he could make. It is a matter of Tito's whole outlook on world politics. You must remember that Khrushchev had taken the initiative of going to Belgrade and trying to compose the differences that had arisen.

MR. FISCHER: *In 1955.*

MR. KENNAN: Yes. And while they had had differences in the meantime, again, over the Party program, nevertheless, Khrushchev was the best friend they had in Moscow, and Tito thought it important at this time to support him. Tito also thought it important to emphasize his own quality as the leader of a socialist state and his usefulness to the others.

MR. FISCHER: *I was going to ask you about any further difficulties you had with the Yugoslavs, but it seems to me they intermesh with the difficulties that arose in your relations with some authorities in the United States so that perhaps you would discuss the whole problem together.*

MR. KENNAN: I might say that after that Belgrade Conference I had very few difficulties with the Yugoslavs. Although a year later, Tito did go to Moscow. He was received by the Supreme Soviet, permitted to address the Supreme Soviet, and given an ovation. Of course, on these occasions and when he came back, naturally moved by this experience, which contrasted very greatly, I may say, with the stinking demonstrations against him here in the United States, he did make statements, again, which were upsetting, which went very far. He even, after that, began to drop the use of the word non-aligned with regard to Yugoslavia's position because the Russians didn't like it, I think.

MR. FISCHER: *One must never forget that, although he's the leader of a nation, he's a Communist.*

MR. KENNAN: Yes. Well, I got to understand all this much better later on and to realize that, while he would make these verbal concessions to the Russians, he had no intention of giving up his independence. Also, that he was not ill-inclined toward either President Kennedy or myself at all, or to us, but he was well aware of the sharp rejection with which he was confronted on the part of the majority opinion here in the Congress. He never forgot this. You can understand that being treated with the greatest of courtesy and cordiality on the Russian side and with insults of one sort or another over here, that this naturally affected his position, too.

Now, this brings me, of course, to this other matter that you raised which is the difficulties experienced here. These difficulties consisted, quite simply, in the fact that at no time during the period that I was Ambassador there did the decisively influential body of opinion in the legislative branch of our government sympathize with the objectives of the President toward Yugoslavia. At no time did it appreciate the advantages of a better relationship with Yugoslavia. On the contrary, the decisive impulse on the part of people in Congress was to use our differences with Yugoslavia—to use Yugoslavia itself—as a sort of a target against which to demonstrate the depth of their own anti-Communism. That is, most of the legislators—the influential ones, the ones who carried the day—valued Yugoslavia principally as something that they could use as a target for hostile sentiments with a view, then, to going back and confronting their electorate and beating their breasts and saying: "Boys, you see how anti-Communist I was; I told them where to head in." It was harder to do this in the case of the Soviet Union because you are always apt to be asked: "Well, what is it you want? A war?" But in the case of Yugoslavia, everybody knew that Yugoslavia was not going to make war on us. And you could use this as a sort of a symbol of Communism and draw a certain amount of political advantage, I suppose, from it. In any case, at no time did the President or myself have support in Congress for the policies we wanted to follow. Not only this but the Congress did persist during this period in taking actions with regard to Yugoslavia which were directly detrimental to our relations.

MR. FISCHER: *What were those actions?*
MR. KENNAN: They were primarily the following: First, in 1962 there was a modification of the aid bill which forbade the President to give any aid to Yugoslavia except when he found that it was vital to the national security. This was troublesome. I, personally, did not favor aid to Yugoslavia. We hardly had any aid programs left at the time I was there, and I folded up the aid mission. All that we had running when I came there as Ambassador was a small technical assistance program which was being folded up when I left, and we had outstanding four or five loans for industrial construction— developmental loans. That is, we had authorized the loans before I went there as Ambassador, and some of these objects were now being constructed during the period that I was there. I thought that we ought not to extend the technical assistance any further; I thought that the surplus wheat should be sold to them only in exceptional circumstances, in drought years such as indeed they had while I was there; I thought that we ought to retain the freedom to give them further loans for industrial development because I thought it undesirable that this sort of assistance should be left entirely to the Russians in Yugoslavia. It wasn't very much; these could be dollar loans. The Yugoslavs were quite prepared to repay the money, and I thought it desirable that they should keep these connections with American industry. So that I had to regret such a clause in the act, first of all, because it really did prevent further developmental loans, but, also, because it tied the hands of the executive branch to a degree which I thought undesirable. I didn't want to see aid extended to the Yugoslavs in general, but I thought that the administration ought to be able to extend it

if it wanted to. It should have this flexibility in order to deal effectively with the Yugoslavs. Furthermore, the very denial of it in a specific paragraph like this was offensive to people who are as sensitive as the Yugoslavs are. And wholly needlessly so, because the Yugoslavs were not asking for aid at this time, and there was absolutely no reason to go out of one's way to put such a clause in the act. During the entire time I was in Yugoslavia, with the exception of the surplus wheat which they simply asked whether they could buy on the going terms, nobody in senior position there ever asked me for any aid from the United States government or voiced an interest in it. Now, why, then, put a special clause in the act like this?

MR. FISCHER: *Doesn't this reflect the relations between President Kennedy and Congress?*
MR. KENNAN: Yes, it did, and I'll go into that in a minute. But much more serious than this clause in the aid bill was a clause which was introduced into the trade bill in 1962 which had the effect of instructing the executive branch to terminate, as soon as practicable, the granting of most favored nation tariff treatment to the Yugoslavs. Now, most favored nations tariff treatment is not especially favorable tariff treatment. It is the normal tariff treatment granted to over eighty or ninety governments in the world. It was treatment which the Yugoslavs had enjoyed at the time when they were a faithful Stalinist satellite. There was absolutely no reason to come along now, when they had liberated themselves from control by the Soviet Union, when they were conducting an independent policy, when they owed us money which they were trying to pay, and inflict this penalty upon them. It would have the effect of raising duties several hundred per cent on a number of Yugoslav commodities, and their exports to us were a paltry fifty million dollars a year. This was nothing to us, and it looked very petty, indeed. I could give them no explanation for it. When Yugoslavs came to me and said: "Look, why is this being done to us?" I would have to say: "I have no knowledge of why it's being done to you."

MR. FISCHER: *Although you knew.*
MR. KENNAN: Well, I couldn't name a reason as to why it should be done now when it wasn't done in Stalin's day. And when they said to me: "Well, what would we have to do to avoid this sort of a penalty?" I was again obliged to say to them: "I don't know what you could do." Now, this was a very difficult position to be in, and I was terribly shocked when I heard that this was being

done. I came home in the summer of 1962 at the time when all this was in the works. At the President's suggestion, I wrote an article for the Sunday edition of the Washington *Post* giving my own reasons why this was not desirable. I saw a number of the legislators in both houses of Congress, called on them, explained my position to them.

MR. FISCHER: *Excuse me, George, how was that suggestion conveyed to you?*
MR. KENNAN: By the President when I called on him personally. He said, "If I were you, I'd go out and. . . ."

MR. FISCHER: *Have you got the date of that?*
MR. KENNAN: Yes, I could tell you when that was. We learned in June of these impulses. That is, that these proposals had been made in Congress to include such clauses in the act. On June 16 the Department released to the press several of my telegrams of protest about this, or the contents of them, summaries of them. On June 30 I, being in London at that time on a trip, received a message from the Department saying that the Department and the White House did not propose to fight the provision in the Foreign Aid Bill, that they were going to concentrate on the most favored nation thing which was much more serious. I was then told to come right home from London, which I did. I published at that time, with the Department's encouragement, a letter in the *New York Times* taking issue with Senator Proxmire, who had made statements about this whole problem which I thought were inaccurate. On July 2 I got home and was received by the President.

MR. FISCHER: *Were you alone with the President?*
MR. KENNAN: Yes. He told me that the next day he wanted me to be over at the White House. He was going to be seeing one or two Senators, and he wanted me to come in casually. He wanted to be able to say to them, "By the way, I think Kennan's waiting out here to see me on another matter. Would you like to talk to him now?" He did bring me in to talk to Senator Hubert Humphrey and to Representative John McCormack.

MR. FISCHER: *What happened on the previous day? What kind of conversation did you have?*
MR. KENNAN: He said on the previous day to me: "I think you ought to state your position for the press." You see, all the way through here . . .

MR. FISCHER: *Did he suggest the Washington* Post?

MR. KENNAN: Yes, he did. The President was reluctant to speak out personally about this. He did not want to take this on as an issue between himself and the Congress. I'm sure that this had to do with the tenuousness of his majority in the election and the fact that he felt he had bigger fish to fry with Congress. He didn't want to have Yugoslavia, which he felt was a fuzzy and unsatisfactory issue, the touchstone of a conflict with a Congressional majority.

MR. FISCHER: *That, perhaps, goes back to the Belgrade Conference, and the impression it made.*

MR. KENNAN: Perhaps. Let me say this: I think he was advised strongly by a portion of his personal advisors in the White House not to touch, publicly, the question of Yugoslavia or the question of international Communism. I think these people told him—I think it was probably Mr. Lawrence O'Brien and others of his internal political advisors—that to do this would get him involved in an argument where he could easily be made to appear soft on Communism, and the others could stand up and pose as the defenders of the national interest. The result was that he didn't want to take this issue up publicly.

MR. FISCHER: *George, did you have any new impression of the President now that he had been in office for some time? Did he look more harried, worried, tired?*

MR. KENNAN: No. I thought he was bearing up very well. One saw a bit the strains of his office, but not seriously. I thought he was carrying on very well. He was very nice to me and very understanding. There was no question he understood entirely my position and the reasons why this was undesirable.

MR. FISCHER: *Did he at that time—the first meeting on July 2—ask you about the general world situation?*

MR. KENNAN: Yes, as I recall it, he did. Then we talked about Yugoslavia, and he said, "Well, I think you ought to state your views publicly and get them out," and so forth. Then he asked me to come back the next day to talk with his Senators. I talked with various other legislators at that time.

MR. FISCHER: *On the next day you saw Senator Humphrey and . . .*

MR. KENNAN: And Representative McCormack in the President's office. That same day he sent me off to see ex-President Eisenhower and to get him to bring his influence to bear on the Republicans in Congress.

MR. FISCHER: *As you presented your case to Humphrey and McCormack, did the President participate at all?*
MR. KENNAN: No, he let me do the talking. He wanted to put me forward.

MR. FISCHER: *He wasn't backing you up or indicating where his sympathies lay?*
MR. KENNAN: Yes. His position vis-à-vis the Senators was that "You know I'm quite impressed with what Kennan says here about this, and I think you ought to hear what he's got to say." This was his position. But he didn't want to say it himself. He sent me, that same day, all the way up to Gettysburg to see President Eisenhower and to get him, if I could, to support my own position with the Republicans in Congress. President Eisenhower agreed with me a hundred per cent, picked up the telephone, called Walter Judd, and said, "Walter, can't you do something to get some sense into this?"

MR. FISCHER: *The last man to ask.*
MR. KENNAN: But, anyway, he, too, was full of sympathy. He said, "This is the problem that I had all the time I was President, and you're absolutely right."

MR. MORRISSEY: *Did he make any other efforts in addition to this call to Congressman Judd?*
MR. KENNAN: Not that I know of. I don't know what he did after I left his office.

MR. FISCHER: *One gets the impression from what you've been saying, George, that President Kennedy was quite conscious of his weak political position.*
MR. KENNAN: I'm sure he was, and I'm sure, also, that he had advisors who urged him very, very strongly not to be pushed by me into taking a position on this. Because this was only the beginning. As the autumn advanced and this thing came to a head, it worked out in a most unfortunate way. In the first place, when I saw all these legislators in July, I was told by the Department of State that "You can talk about aid yourself, but leave the most favored nation issue alone because we think we're going to get a quiet understanding that this will be removed if we don't make a public issue of it." So I didn't press this any further then and went back to my post. To my horror in September on the eighteenth we got news . . .

MR. FISCHER: *That's what year?*
MR. KENNAN: '62. All this was in the summer and fall of '62. We got news that

the House Appropriations Subcommittee had taken affirmative action on this most favored nations clause and . . .

MR. FISCHER: *Affirmative action aimed against you . . .*
MR. KENNAN: Yes, they wanted to embody this in the bill: the clause denying most favored nation treatment to Yugoslavia. And on September 27 this whole thing came to a head. Contrary to the assurances we had had in Belgrade from the Department of State, the conferees of the two houses agreed to vote on this amendment; they agreed to accept it. We had hoped that the Senate would throw it out, but they didn't. Led by Representative [Wilbur] Mills of the House Ways and Means Committee, to whom I had explained this when I was back in Washington, the conferees, nevertheless accepted the clause.

MR. FISCHER: *Did you see Mills at the suggestion of the President?*
MR. KENNAN: I can't remember whether it was specifically at his suggestion or not, but it was in the line of calls that he wanted me to make down there. The conferees accepted this amendment which meant it was bound to go through. This worked out in the worst possible way because what happened that day . . . This was the day, anyway, we got the news that they had accepted it—the 27th of September. We got the news in the morning. I had the unpleasant duty of going right down to the Foreign Office to tell the Yugoslavs of this because I knew it would be a serious blow to our relations. It came to them as an absolutely gratuitous act of hostility, a slap in the face, and one that I couldn't explain to them in any way. It put me in a very difficult position. That afternoon I received a call from Fred Dutton, who was Assistant Secretary of State in charge of Congressional Relations. It was a call that came over the open long distance telephone so that the Yugoslavs were, of course, listening. Dutton said, in effect, "George, we're all terribly distressed about what has occurred here, and there's only one thing that could stop it at this point, or do any good. And that would be if you would appeal personally by telephone directly to the President." Now I point out that this statement, coming over the long distance telephone with the Yugoslavs listening, left me holding the bag for the entire most favored nation treatment problem, and I had no choice, then, but to call the President. So I did call him that evening and said to him, [In effect, I can't remember the exact words, of course.] "This is most unfortunate and is going to have a most destructive effect on our relations with these people. I have to tell you that this places in jeopardy my success

and my whole mission out here." The President said, "Mr. Ambassador, I think you ought to talk to Mr. Mills, and, if you don't mind, I'm going to transfer this call to him."

MR. FISCHER: *That was all the conversation? You began by stating your point of view, and he gave you no other reply?*

MR. KENNAN: That is right. He gave me no other reply and said he would have the call transferred to Mr. Mills. I got Mr. Mills. Anticipating something of this sort, I had written out what I wanted to say to him. Afterwards I called the Department of State on the telephone, repeated this statement to the Department of State, asked them to give it in writing to Mr. Mills in addition to the oral expression of it I had given. The statement was as follows, and I lay considerable weight on this because it was all I could do in the circumstances. I said the following to Mr. Mills: "I understand that the House-Senate conferees are considering the adoption in the trade bill of an amendment that would deny most favored nation treatment to Yugoslavia. Speaking in my official capacity as Ambassador in Belgrade and against the background of thirty-five years of experience with the affairs of Eastern Europe, I must give it as my considered judgment that such an amendment coming at the present time and in present circumstances would be unnecessary, uncalled for, and injurious to United States interests. It would be taken, not only in Yugoslavia but throughout this part of the world, as evidence of a petty and vindictive spirit unworthy of a country of our stature and responsibility. This judgment has the concurrence of every officer in this mission. If the amendment is adopted, it will be in disregard of the most earnest and serious advice we are capable of giving." This, too, of course, was heard by the Yugoslavs.

MR. FISCHER: *Representative Mills knew that the President had transferred the call?*

MR. KENNAN: He knew that the President had transferred the call. He didn't reply definitely to this except that "I think it's too late to make any change," and I never heard from him again; the amendment went through. This wasn't all. We were informed, and the Yugoslavs were given the impression, that, when the President signed the bill, he would voice his own discontent at least with this amendment. I learned two or three days later in a message from Bundy that, when the President signed the bill, he failed to voice any discontent with the amendment. On the other hand he did express his admiration for Mr. Mills as a statesman and his appreciation for the work that Mr. Mills had done on this bill. This, of course, added to the sting so far as the Yugoslavs were concerned.

MR. FISCHER: *George, I get the impression, therefore, that you're rather critical of the President for his failure to support you on this matter.*
MR. KENNAN: You know, I think it's a sign of the President's great human qualities that I never actually felt bitter against him for this. I felt bitter about the situation. I felt completely let down, and I felt that my own personal usefulness in Belgrade was destroyed by this: my helplessness had been documented to the Yugoslavs, and it couldn't have been made clearer to them that the utmost that I could do, that my entire personal influence—everything I stood for, everything I represented, all the years of experience I had had in this field—didn't carry that much with the decisive forces in the Congress of the United States. I sat down a day or two later and drafted a letter to Mac Bundy which I never sent, but which would give you an idea from certain passages in it of how I felt, and how I felt with regard to the President here.

MR. FISCHER: *Could you read those passages please?*
MR. KENNAN: I referred to his message in which he explained the circumstances surrounding the signing of the bill by the President, and I said, "I have read it with appreciation for your courtesy and frankness in letting me know of these circumstances and with sympathy for the President in what has obviously been for him an extremely difficult situation. I have no desire to belittle the difficulty of the choice with which he has been confronted. Nevertheless, the fact remains that his choice fell as it did on this crucial occasion. The Yugoslav reaction has been as predicted. We were warned that this would affect our relations adversely. And I am afraid that I have to ask myself all over again what implications this bears for my own personal position and whether, in particular, I could and should attempt to remain here as the exponent of a line of conduct on the part of our government which did not, to be sure, flow from any initiative of the executive branch, but in which, for internal political reasons, it has found it necessary to acquiesce, and of which I myself am known to disapprove profoundly." This was the situation, and I offered to submit my resignation then and urged the President to accept it but to ask me to remain temporarily at my post as a custodian until he could make . . .

MR. FISCHER: *Did you write to the President?*
MR. KENNAN: I wired.

MR. FISCHER: *You wired to the President?*
MR. KENNAN: But the President didn't want to do this.

MR. FISCHER: *How do you know this? Did he write to you?*
MR. KENNAN: I don't have the correspondence here, but I know that I wired
offering to resign at that time. I had some sort of reply saying that the President didn't want me to do this—that he wanted me to reconsider. I can remember taking a long, long walk all by myself on the Sunday morning after
that week, fighting with myself as to whether to resign or not. My wife, with
good sense, persuaded me not to and said it would seem abrupt, and it would
seem a demonstration against the President, and you don't want to do that.
So I didn't. But, when I came home in January of 1963, about three months
later, I told both the President and the Secretary of State that I would hope
to resume my academic work the following fall. That meant that I left the
government service about nine or ten months after this episode, at a time
when the public had largely forgotten about it and didn't take it as a demonstration against the President. Since you asked me whether this caused me any
bitterness against the President, I'd like to read to you one or two other communications that passed between us. In the first place on July 17, 1963, about
ten days before I finally left Yugoslavia, the President wrote me as follows:
"Dear Mr. Ambassador: It is with deep regret that I accept your resignation as
Ambassador to Yugoslavia on a date to be determined. Your departure from
the service of the government will be a great loss, but I understand your desire
to return to your work at the Institute of Advanced Studies at Princeton. Your
insights and advice have at all times proved of value to us in shaping our
foreign policy, and I have profited, as well, from your analyses and interpreta-
tions of events. The United States has been fortunate in having you as its
Ambassador to Yugoslavia, and I am sincerely grateful that you were willing
to respond to my request that you undertake this mission. As you return to
academic life, you have my warm thanks and best wishes for the future." So
much for the letter. I had the impression that the President completely understood what he did to me, and I, on the other hand, completely understood
why he had to do it. It was quite clear to me that Yugoslavia was not worth a
conflict between him and the Congress which might have gummed up his
whole civil rights program and other great undertakings here of domestic legislation. This was a tragic situation, and I think both of us came out of it

entirely without bitterness. On October 22, 1963, two or three months after
I returned to this country and after I had laid down my functions as Ambassador, I wrote the President a hand-written note which I sent to him through
Bundy. I didn't even have it typed. It read as follows: "Dear Mr. President: You
get many brickbats, and of those who say approving and encouraging things
not all are pure of motive. I am now fully retired and a candidate for neither
elective nor appointive office. I think, therefore, that my sincerity may be
credited if I take this means to speak a word of encouragement. I am full of
admiration, both as a historian and as a person with diplomatic experience,
for the manner in which you have addressed yourself to the problems of
foreign policy with which I am familiar. I don't think we have seen a better
standard of statesmanship in the White House in the present century. I hope
you will continue to be of good heart and allow yourself to be discouraged
neither by the appalling pressures of your office nor by the obtuseness and
obstruction you encounter in another branch of the government. Please know
that I and many others are deeply grateful for the courage and patience and
perception with which you carry on. Very sincerely yours . . ." I had a reply
from him dated October 28, 1963, which I think was very shortly . . .

MR. FISCHER: *Just a month before he was . . .*
MR. MORRISSEY: October the 22 was exactly a month before the assassination.
MR. KENNAN: Well, this was October 28, saying, "Dear George, [This is the
first time he had addressed me in this way.] Your handwritten note of October
22 is a letter I will keep nearby for reference and reenforcement on hard days.
It is a great encouragement to have the support of a diplomat and historian of
your quality, and it was uncommonly thoughtful for you to write me in this
personal way." He also referred here to a note I had written him about the
Tito visit.

This was pretty much the story with regard to Yugoslavia. It was, as I say,
a tragic situation. These people in Congress could not have been more wrong;
this was stupid. It had the effect of pushing the Yugoslavs back into the arms
of the bloc. I must say that I resented very deeply, and the President knew
this, the pressures that were brought to bear in this direction on the part of
the Congress, and I felt very strongly about it. The Yugoslavs had one of the
three strongest armies in Europe not under Soviet control. For fifteen years
they had had nothing to do with the Red Army; they had not even bought

military equipment from Russia; they had no Soviet military missions in Yugo-slavia; and the temper of the Yugoslav armed forces was strongly pro-American. This was a situation which was of benefit to us, of benefit to stability in that area of the Balkans and the Adriatic, and important to the maintenance of the peace of Europe. As a result of this situation, the Russians, who ten or fifteen years earlier had had a military presence along eight hundred miles of the Adriatic coast—all the way from Trieste down to the southern border of Albania—were now present nowhere on the Adriatic coast. The Italians had benefited enormously by this as a NATO country; so had the Greeks. Relations between Italy and Yugoslavia were better than they had ever been in history. This was, as I say, a situation of greatest value to NATO. To take the position, as men in Congress now did; "Aw, tell them we don't care what happens to 'em. They can go back to Moscow. They're a lot of damned Communists, aren't they?"—this was the sort of talk I got—was simply so irresponsible and so childish that I felt very strongly about the impropriety of it, and I was perfectly willing to go out and leave my job over this issue. I am not sure to this day that the President was right not to make this an issue. I only say that I understood the cruelty of his choice. I thought that, if he failed in those years when I was associated with him in this way—if he failed anywhere in his approach to foreign policy—it was in the fact that he did not do enough to try to teach the American public the basic facts about the world. He did give the one speech of June, I think, 1963 at American University in Washington which was important and was constructive. I thought this was fine, but one speech is not enough. I think he should have done more. On the other hand I was always very much aware that I was not in a good position to judge his internal political problems and that, therefore, I ought to reserve judgment about this.

MR. FISCHER: *George, in view of this criticism, what prompted you to write that article of praise for his conduct of international affairs in general?*
MR. KENNAN: Do you mean this letter?

MR. FISCHER: *Yes, the letter, your letter.*
MR. KENNAN: I thought that in what he did in the White House, to the extent he was permitted to do it by Congress, that this was the best, as I said, that I could think of.

MR. FISCHER: *What specifically? For instance, the Cuban missile crisis?*

MR. KENNAN: The way in which he handled that. The test ban agreement. In general, his handling of foreign statesmen, his handling of himself on his visits to Europe—his willingness to listen; above all, his willingness to seek advice, to find out about things—all of this seemed to me to be first rate, and I was much impressed by his handling of Tito.

MR. FISCHER: *Would you tell us about that, and what was the date?*
MR. KENNAN: After I had returned to Princeton here, I received one day a request by telephone from the White House or from the State Department, I can't remember which, saying that the President would like Mrs. Kennan and myself to go down to Williamsburg and to greet the Tito party when they came to this country because nobody else had yet been appointed as Ambassador to Yugoslavia, and we knew Tito and his wife well. The President wanted me to do this as a favor to him, so I immediately assented. Mrs. Kennan and I did go down there to Williamsburg. We met President Tito. We escorted him up to Washington and were present at the luncheon that the President gave for him. I was, however, not present at Tito's interview with the President because I was no longer formally the Ambassador. I wrote the President afterwards giving him some of my impressions of what Tito had thought of the visit, of his reactions to it. In this same letter of October 28, in which he acknowledged my handwritten note of encouragement to him, he added a paragraph saying, "I also have your note about the Tito visit. I must say I think it went very well, and we are all grateful to you for your help in getting the tone right and in handling the Princeton leg of the visit." Tito, I may say, later came up here to Princeton, and here, too, I participated as I think you did. Didn't you?

MR. FISCHER: *No, I wasn't here.*
MR. KENNAN: You weren't here. I participated in greeting him here, again. He was rather amused that I popped up both in the official world and in the academic world as one of his hosts. He had a very pleasant day in Princeton, and the President appreciated that. The President, I may say, was wonderful on that occasion of the Tito visit. The Tito visit was a most difficult thing to arrange. The anti-Yugoslav forces in this country were determined to make every conceivable trouble for the visit, to do everything they could do. And believe me, they did! It was all right at Williamsburg, and we had no difficulty there because things were controlled down there. But we had to bring Tito up

by helicopter from Williamsburg to the White House lawn in order to keep him from going through the Washington streets. Even then there were crowds of people stationed as near as they could get to the White House lawn, and you could hear them jeering and screaming. There were people in Nazi uniforms demonstrating right across the street from the White House, and to his dying day Tito will never understand why people in Nazi uniforms should have been permitted to demonstrate against him, an allied chief of state from the war-time period, across the street from the White House. But this was nothing compared to what happened in New York, which was absolutely shameful! He and his party were put up in the Waldorf Astoria Towers. It was worse than picketing; the building was surrounded day and night by people in a high state of physical fury—most, I think, not even citizens of our country. Nobody knows. They were obviously Croatians, Serbs. The camped in the Coffee Shop there. The women of the Yugoslav delegation included some very fine and proud women who had been in the partisan movement themselves—wives of some of these officials—could not go down in the Coffee Shop without having these people get up on their chairs and hiss at them and call them prostitutes. Three of the Yugoslavs were beaten up trying to leave the building. The New York police obviously sympathized with the demonstrators, and these people were simply prisoners up there in this tower and miserably unhappy. It was a very disturbing thing and left me with the impression that it's high time this country took measures to assure polite, decent, courteous treatment of foreign heads of state when they visit the country. But this was simply the atmosphere of the visit.

The President, himself, talked to me the day before. (On my way down there I called on him.) He asked me to draw up for him a text of something he could say in the way of a public toast at the luncheon for Tito. I did draw up a statement; he used it—he drew on it, but he edited it, threw in some things of his own, and I thought he had improved perceptibly, with his own deft and oblique touch, on what I had written.

MR. FISCHER: *Can you say specifically what modifications he made?*
MR. KENNAN: No. I can't remember that, but I remember that I was full of admiration and felt that he had improved greatly on what I had written.

MR. FISCHER: *Well, that's quite an achievement.*
MR. KENNAN: I'm not so easily convinced of this sort of thing, but I felt that

he had given it his inimitable touch. He carried the whole luncheon off beautifully without saying too much, without saying fulsome things that could be used against him, but at the same time without ever being anything else than courteous and hospitable toward his guest.

MR. FISCHER: *That was the last time you saw him?*
MR. KENNAN: That was the last time I saw him. I didn't have a chance to talk to him personally that day at the luncheon for any length of time. When I saw him the day before, that was the last time I talked to him personally. As far as I can recall, the last thing he said to me was, "George, I hope you'll keep on talking." This is one of the reasons why, since his assassination, I have tried to speak occasionally, publicly, on public problems, even though it has caused difficulty with my academic work here.

MR. FISCHER: *Have you any assessment of his evolution—development—during the presidency?*
MR. KENNAN: Yes. I felt that he grew greatly in his job, and that the man that I saw, for instance, on the occasion of this Tito visit and when I returned from Yugoslavia, was a man who was already considerably greater in stature, more mature, more measured in his judgments, more seasoned than the man I had seen initially.

MR. FISCHER: *When you flew down from New York to Washington?*
MR. KENNAN: Yes. I felt that he was getting a grasp of his tasks; that things might have been quite different in his second term: that, had he been elected with a larger majority and had he had better support in Congress, he would have gone on, then, to a more constructive phase of his own foreign policy. For example, I was very disappointed when I read the account, which I was permitted to do, of his Vienna meeting and discussion with Khrushchev. I was shown the verbatim account of that.

MR. FISCHER: *That was very early—in June, 1961.*
MR. KENNAN: In June 1961, just after I had gone to Yugoslavia. I was actually telegraphed from Washington and told to go to Paris; the President, I think, wanted me to see the text of this. I felt that he had not acquitted himself well on this occasion and that he had permitted Khrushchev to say many things which should have been challenged right there on the spot. But he, feeling his way, preferred to let Khrushchev talk and not to rebut any of this. I think

this was a mistake. I think it definitely misled Khrushchev; I think Khrushchev failed to realize on that occasion what a man he was up against and, also, thought that he'd gotten away with many of these talking points; that he had placed President Kennedy in a state of confusion where he had nothing to say in return.

MR. FISCHER: *That was June 1961. Do you think this might have had some influence on Khrushchev's attitude towards Cuba and placement of the missiles there?*
MR. KENNAN: Yes, I do, although I have never personally been satisfied that we can be sure that it was Khrushchev who wanted most to do this. I think there is a possibility that in this action of the Soviet government Khrushchev was pressed by military circles in the Soviet Union and others, and that it went beyond what he, himself, might have approved.

MR. FISCHER: *But whoever it was—the military or others—would have known about Khrushchev's impression of Kennedy from that first interview in Vienna.*
MR. KENNAN: That's correct. I did feel that this was . . .

MR. FISCHER: *Would have encouraged an aggressive spirit on the part of the Soviets.*
MR. KENNAN: I think so. I think they thought that this is a tongue-tied young man who's not forceful and who doesn't have ideas of his own; they felt that they could get away with something.

MR. FISCHER: *Don't you think he made up for it in his conduct of the Cuban missile crisis?*
MR. KENNAN: Yes. I thought this was masterful. And I think they realized, too, how well this was handled.

MR. FISCHER: *In other words in effect, although not deliberately, Kennedy trapped them.*
MR. KENNAN: Yes. He was, I felt, strangely tongue-tied in this interview with Khrushchev, and numbers of these typical, characteristic Communist exaggerations and false accusations were simply let pass, you see, instead of being replied to—being rebutted.

MR. FISCHER: *It was because he was young in office.*
MR. KENNAN: Yes. He was feeling his way. I didn't feel, you know, that he was initially firm in his ideas of what he wanted to do about the Communist problem. I think he was always bothered by the strong anti-Communist sentiment in Congress; so were some of his advisors. The terrible difficulty here was that it seemed in those years as though there was a certain political dividend always

to be reaped here at home, in terms of internal politics, by a strong and flamboyant anti-Communist demonstrative posture. People on the legislative side of the government were constantly taking advantage of this. While the President did not do this himself, it was just forceful enough to make him unwilling to get pressed onto the other side of such a posture. In other words, he didn't want other people to be able to say that he was in favor of Communism.

I would like to emphasize again if I might, although this reverts to what I've said before about relations with Yugoslavia, the difficulty that this made for us in Yugoslavia. These strong anti-Communist pressures—Communist pressures that dated from the days of Senator McCarthy and all that—they interfered very greatly with our relations with Yugoslavia. You must remember that we had in this country, living peacefully in California, the man who had been the Minister of the Interior in the Nazi Croatian government—the Pavelíc government—which had declared war on us together with the Nazis in 1941, which had destroyed its own Jews at Hitler's instructions, and which had carried out appalling atrocities together with the Nazis against the Serbs and the Moslem inhabitants of the Nazi Croatia at that time. Now, the man who was directly responsible for all these atrocities, a man by the name of Artyuković, had entered this country illegally under a false name. Nevertheless, he had never been deported, and he was still, as I say, comfortably living out there in California and commanding, apparently, a good deal of political influence in the Congress. The Yugoslavs resented this intensely and, I must say, with a great deal of justification. This was absolutely wrong. The man had been able to remain in this country simply due to political pull. You see how these pressures interfere with our relations with these people. It wasn't that the Yugoslav position was perfect; it wasn't that they were always right; it wasn't that we didn't have arguments with them—we did. But our own position was weakened by the fact that we simply were unable to take a consistent position toward Yugoslavia due to the fact that the legislative branch was so amenable—so vulnerable—to this sort of internal political pressure.

MR. FISCHER: *George, one final question about a purely technical, or administrative, aspect of our diplomacy: Does it seem to you that the President had his own little State Department in the White House; that he was his own Secretary of State to some extent?*
MR. KENNAN: I thought increasingly less so as he went along. You know, a very remarkable thing about my own mission in Yugoslavia was that I never

had the impression that the Secretary of State was in any way interested in my problems or my affairs or entered into the exchanges I had with Washington in any way. The same was true of Mr. [George] Ball. I felt that Mr. Ball and the Secretary were interested in entirely different things; that they regarded this appointment as an appointment by Mr. Kennedy; they would not have selected me, and they were not interested in what happened to me. They, too, agreed that these Congressional actions were unfortunate. They opposed them publicly more than the President did, but very little, too. On the other hand, they didn't figure in the equation in any way, shape, or form. Nobody, as far as I could see, senior to [William R.] Bill Tyler, who was the head of the European Office in the State Department, was particularly interested in my problems there. I had my differences with the Department of State just on the opposite side; I wanted the Department of State to be tougher with the Yugoslavs about questions of aid than the Department was inclined to be. I had told them many times when I came home at the end of my stay in Yugoslavia that my position was made impossible there because the only way to deal with the Yugoslavs was through a combination of the carrot and the stick; the Congress wouldn't hear of the carrot, and the Department of State wouldn't hear of the stick. The Yugoslavs knew this and knew that neither could anything good be done for them, because of Congressional objections, nor could anything be done that would injure them, because the State Department would veto it. So the Ambassador was paralyzed.

MR. FISCHER: *You have every right to be bitter towards the Kennedy Administration, and, yet, I sense that you have no animosity or hard feelings towards the President himself. Is there anything in his personality that would explain it?*
MR. KENNAN: I think that there was. In the first place, here he was. He was relatively young. He was terribly alone with this loneliness that is known only to people in supreme position. I realized this. When I came home and saw him there in his room—that bedroom of his upstairs in the White House—and realized the pressures that were brought to bear against him, realized even what it meant to him to take an hour out to sit down in his rocking chair and talk with me, I always was aware that I must not look at his position from the standpoint of my problems. Great as they seemed to me, these were only a tiny portion of the problems that he had. His own decency toward me, his readiness to listen, convinced me that, if he was unable to support me, it was

not for lack of desire on his part; it was because he thought that, on balance, this was the politically desirable thing to do; that to him, as to every man in senior political position, politics was the art of the possible, and he could only do those things that seemed to him, on balance, correct. I had nothing but sympathy for him. I was sorry that it was myself when he was obliged in a way to destroy, and it worked out very unfortunately. I must say, I blamed for this, almost more, the Congressional liaison people in the Department of State who time after time let us down and gave us no opportunity to state our views until the very last moment, when something catastrophic had already happened.

It was not only, I must say, these things that I told you about. There was another episode which was very unfortunate. Before I left for my post, I wrote a long letter. I can't remember whether it was to Tommie Thompson or to the Secretary or to Bundy or to whom it was, but it was a long letter, I think to Bundy, about the Captive Nations Resolution which was still on the books and which I considered to be very unfortunate from the standpoint of our relations with Russia and our relations with Yugoslavia. I begged that the President at least refrain in that year, which was 1961, from announcing Captive Nations Week. About a week before this time came, I got a telegram saying that the President was not going to announce Captive Nations Week. I learned later that this same thing was told orally to the Yugoslav Embassy in Washington. This was, as I recall it, in June 1961 just in the very early stages of his Administration. This would have been taken by the Yugoslavs . . .

MR. FISCHER: *Was that on the eve of his interview with Khrushchev in Vienna or do you know? It might have been in that connection.*

MR. KENNAN: I can't remember whether it was just before or just after. I'm inclined to think it must have been just after.

We were very much encouraged by this, and so were the Yugoslavs. We had been told again, the day before, that no such announcement would be made, and we were given suggestions as how to explain this to the press if they asked. On the day that the announcement was due, we received a telegram in the morning to the effect that they greatly regretted, but this decision had been reconsidered, and the President was going to announce this. Somebody had twisted his arm overnight in Congress. Now, this Captive Nations Resolution is a disgraceful thing. It commits us not only to the liberation of a great many peoples to whose liberation we ought not to be committed for various reasons but also to the liberation of two that have no existence in fact at all—something called Kazakhia, and something called Ude-Ural. A professor of Ukrainian origin at Marquette University in Milwaukee has publicly boasted that he wrote every word of the Captive Nations Resolution. I felt that it was a shocking thing that our government should be committed to an absurd statement of this sort; one that didn't represent United States' interests at all, but the interests of certain exile groups over here. The fact that this was knocked out at the last moment was again difficult for me. I had said to the Yugoslavs—I had said before—"You watch. This year the President's not going to announce this." You can see what a position this left me in.

MR. FISCHER: *Did the U.S. government make any use of your vast Soviet background while you were in Yugoslavia in those years?*
MR. KENNAN: Initially, the President did: in consulting me as we've already gone over in the early stages of his Administration. The State Department did a bit, initially, but rather under my own encouragement. I pointed out, I think, myself to the Secretary of State that I had the opportunity of talking under four eyes, so to speak, without an interpreter or anybody else present, with my Soviet colleague in Belgrade.

MR. FISCHER: *In Russian.*
MR. KENNAN: In Russian, and without the world press knowing anything about our meetings. There was no American press to speak of in Belgrade those days, and they didn't shadow me or anything like that; so that it was perfectly easy for me to walk right over from my home to the Soviet Ambassador's home and sit down with him in his own living room, and the two of us talked together without any interference. I pointed out that this might be of value to the Department and that, if there were any subjects on which they would like me to draw him out or to express our point of view, I would be glad to know them and to conduct such discussions. Obviously, this had to be done very secretly. I was authorized to talk with him and got telegrams of instruction saying what to say to him on two subjects: on Laos and on Berlin. The conversations on Laos were a little difficult for me because I was never informed of the background, which is always a mistake. If you want a man to negotiate, you should give him the whole background. Nevertheless, these did appear to have a certain success, and I attribute the subsequent quietness of the Laotian

situation, in part, to these discussions. I had a feeling that we made progress; that certain things were said on both sides which served to relieve the fears of the other side and that, in effect, both sides agreed to lay off if the other didn't agitate this problem too much. As you noticed, the Laotian thing didn't bother us so much in the coming year.

So far as Berlin is concerned, we were just starting to get going with these discussions. We'd had two or three. It was perfectly evident that in his replies to me [Aleksey Alekseyevich] Yepishev was speaking directly for Khrushchev. I was confident that some of the things said would never have been said except in an absolutely private conversation like this. But as of June 1961, only a month or two after I arrived there, I ceased to get instructions; they didn't want me to see him any more.

MR. FISCHER: *This was at the beginning of your stay.*

MR. KENNAN: Yes, and this channel was never used again. I attribute this decision, not to the President, but to the Secretary of State, who, I think, didn't like private conversations. Neither he nor Ball wanted me talking with anyone about Berlin; they were terrified of this because they thought that, if it ever came out, it would be, I think, objectionable to the Adenauer government. Not only this, but I think, in a way, they didn't really want any agreement about Berlin. They didn't want an agreement; they wanted the Russians to simply desist and capitulate, but they didn't want to discuss it with them.

I always felt that it was a great shame that this channel was allowed to die, because they will not have found a better one. You see, if you have other people doing this, in the first place, if it's done in the big capitals, there's always the danger the press gets a hold of it, and, secondly, if they're people who don't know Russian, you have to have interpreters present, and that already ruins the complete privacy of it. The Ambassador in Moscow cannot do it—I can assure you of this—because the moment he goes down to the Foreign Office the room is wired, and everything is written down. This becomes a formal approach. So you can't try out anything that way. It was a disappointment to me—a double disappointment—because

[Portions omitted because of classification restrictions]

MR. FISCHER: *Another question, George. How did the Yugoslavs—the leaders and the people—take the Cuban missile crisis in October 1962?*

MR. KENNAN: I was not there at the moment it happened. I was in Milan on a short holiday. We had the Embassy Cadillac up there with our Moslem chauffeur, and he made the 700 miles back from Milan to Belgrade, as I remember it, in eleven hours. If you know Yugoslav roads. . . . [Laughter.]

MR. FISCHER: *Yes, that's a record.*
MR. KENNAN: A real record getting me back there. They, I think, understood our position on the removal of the missiles and disapproved of the stationing of the missiles there. Not only this, but the Yugoslavs did not have happy relations with [Fidel] Castro. They didn't like him. They had found a number of points of bitter disagreement and argument in their own attempts to handle their own relations with Castro so that they were not, perhaps, as moved as much by sympathy for the Cubans as they might otherwise have been. What did bother them was the restrictions afterward on shipping to Cuba. This was a matter of utmost delicacy and could, again, have wrecked our relations because they felt very strongly that it was their right to send their ships to any other country they wanted to send them to. Not only this, but then we had trouble because at that time the American Maritime Union here began to refuse to load or unload any Yugoslav ship in our ports. We had a lot of difficulty over that. This was where . . .

MR. FISCHER: *When you say "they," could you state whether you had any conversation with somebody in the Foreign Office?*
MR. KENNAN: Yes, I discussed this with them on many occasions, and they . . .

MR. FISCHER: *No, I mean their response to the Cuban missile crisis. Did you talk to any Minister or. . . .*
MR. KENNAN: No. Not that I can specifically recall. I only remember that their attitude toward the actual conflict between the Russians and ourselves over these missiles was very reserved. They didn't want to get into this.

MR. FISCHER: *Did anybody appreciate the skill with which Kennedy had handled this?*
MR. KENNAN: Yes, they did. They appreciated the fact that he gave the Russians a way out before he pressed them. They respected this. It was the pressures engendered, again in the legislative branch, over Cuba that caused them difficulty rather than what the President did. But they always warned me that, if we were to provoke a real armed conflict with the Cubans, they would have to come down on the Cuban side.

MR. FISCHER: *But you can't remember that you had any conversation with a Yugoslav official who gave you an appreciation of the President's conduct of that Cuban missile crisis?*
MR. KENNAN: No. I can't.

MR. FISCHER: *What did the press say? Do you remember?*
MR. KENNAN: The press were, I think, rather hostile to us, but also did not approve of the Soviet action in putting the missiles there. They didn't approve of our blockade, but they didn't approve of putting the missiles in there. I may say that I had many arguments with the Yugoslav press and even wrote letters protesting against some of the things they said about world affairs. But there was this great difference between my situation in this respect and the situation of chiefs of missions in the regular bloc countries—in the Soviet Union and the satellite countries—namely that, when I had protested about something they wrote about Vietnam, somebody called me up and said, "Wouldn't you like to sit down with some of the leading Yugoslav editors of an evening and talk about these things?" I said I'd be delighted. So I was asked by their Chief of Information to a dinner at a restaurant way up there on the hill one evening. I took two or three of the Serbo-Croatian speaking officers from our mission; we went up there, and we had a very pleasant evening and a lively, good, friendly—but sharp—discussion all evening over these things with no hard feelings, everybody speaking his mind openly. This would have been impossible in Moscow.

MR. FISCHER: *Of course.*
MR. KENNAN: So that even where we had these differences, I couldn't complain. I was so well treated, in fact, by these people that it was a double source of chagrin to me that I had to dish out such treatment to them in return.

MR. FISCHER: *Did Tito ever talk to you about Castro?*
MR. KENNAN: I believe that he did mention it to me once. He was reserved, again, because he didn't want to say much against Castro. But I did not fail to notice (and I wish the American press had noticed) that he did not visit Cuba when he came to this side of the water; he came to Washington, but he did not come to Cuba although the American press reported, utterly erroneously, that he was going to go there. But this was a sensitive issue, and we could have had—we still could have—a great deal of trouble with them over Cuba.

MR. FISCHER: *Dr. Morrissey, do you have any questions?*

MR. MORRISSEY: *This question about did you have any intimations of Khrushchev's decreasing security in the Kremlin. Could you comment on that?*

MR. KENNAN: Yes. The Yugoslavs told me on many occasions that Khrushchev was faced with a strong opposition within his own establishment. I have somewhere here the text of a message that I sent after a conversation with the Soviet Ambassador in which I think this was mentioned.

[tape recorder turned off—resumes]

MR. KENNAN: No. Actually, on looking it over I see that this did not come up in this particular talk. But both from Yepishev and from the Yugoslavs I repeatedly was given the assurance that there was a divisive situation in the high policy-making echelons of the Soviet government; that Khrushchev was faced with fairly strong opposition from hard-liners who were not completely sold on the Chinese line or anything like that, but who wanted to see a hard line taken toward us. The same, of course, was true within the Yugoslav government. There were differences of opinion there.

MR. FISCHER: *George, I'm sure there was a difference of opinion in the Presidium of the Soviet Communist Party, and we know that in the final analysis Khrushchev was dismissed, but I wonder whether Tito and Yepishev were not talking to you knowing that you would report this to some authority in the United States with the view of moderating our pressures on Khrushchev and thereby strengthening his hand.*

MR. KENNAN: I think this is quite possible, and I think this is probably what people felt in Washington. But I also think there was something to it.

MR. FISCHER: *Oh yes! I'm not denying that there was something to it.*

MR. KENNAN: One of the objections I had to our policy from the time of the U-2 on was that I felt that we did not dangle enough in the way of favorable prospects before the Soviet government to support Khrushchev in his coexistence like with us, and that we created a situation in which he had to scurry for cover by talking a very, very tough line toward us. This was visible right at the time of the U-2.

MR. FISCHER: *George, it occurs to me that we haven't discussed one problem that was certainly faced by President Kennedy. And that was the German problem. How do you explain this shift in Tito's attitude towards Germany? At one time—certainly in 1952—*

when I talked to him (I had two interviews with him), he said that he had no objection to a strong, armed Germany. Later, of course, his attitude changed.

MR. KENNAN: Well, you know, by the end of the fifties he had no military fear of the Soviet Union any more because the atmosphere was quite different; Khrushchev had taken a different attitude toward him. On the other hand, he was deeply worried by what we had done between 1952 and 1962 in the way of rearming western Germany. Not only this, but he and the other Yugoslavs were very sensitive to two things in their relations with Germany: One was the activities in Germany of the Yugoslav exiles which were very similar to those of the exiles in this country. In fact, while I was in Belgrade, on one Sunday, those exiles attacked the Yugoslav mission in Bonn, killed one of its employees, and attacked it in a way that threatened the safety of the children in the mission. The Yugoslavs were absolutely fit to be tied over this; that this should happen to them in Germany which was a defeated country. They'd been an allied mission, and they felt very strongly about this.

In addition to this, they couldn't get very far in their commercial talks with the Germans. They wanted to talk about the Common Market and their commercial problems; the Germans were very offish toward them—the Adenauer government—for reasons very similar to the reasons for the conduct and attitude of our Congress. The religious issues played a strong part with the Adenauer government, as you can imagine, and of course, also, the Hallstein Doctrine. I made one trip to Bonn to argue with the German Foreign Office a bit about this because the Yugoslavs had no representative there and couldn't talk to them. I did try to persuade them how useful it would be to encourage the Yugoslavs, who already had about 70 percent of their trade with the West, to feel that they were welcome in economic relations with the West. But I couldn't get very far with Bonn either. They were not very responsive. I would say the German problem was comparable to the hostility in our own Congress as among the factors persuading Tito and his associates that they had little to hope for in their relations with the West.

MR. MORRISSEY: *You mentioned early in the interview that you endorsed John Kennedy in the 1960 campaign.*

MR. KENNAN: Yes. You know, I don't recall doing that. He mentions it, and since I think that he was probably quite accurate in his political responses, I have no doubt that I did. But I don't remember doing it. I didn't take any active part in the campaign. I had been. . . . Let's see, when Adlai Stevenson ran the second time for the presidency, I headed the Stevenson for President organization here in New Jersey. So I was on record at least as being a pro-Stevenson person, and I once did register for election to the House of Representatives out in Pennsylvania on the Democratic ticket but was obliged to withdraw for personal financial reasons. I discovered that I couldn't get any more salary or support either from the Institute here or the Rockefeller Foundation if I became a candidate for public office, which I thought was profoundly wrong, really, because I think that it should be regarded as a normal duty of citizenship—to run if you're asked, as I was, for public office. You shouldn't be financially penalized for it. But these were the only contacts I had had with political life prior to that time, and I don't remember in what way I endorsed Mr. Kennedy's candidacy. I certainly, if asked, would have done it.

MR. MORRISSEY: *Early in the Kennedy Administration a crisis desk was established in the State Department to deal with crises that arose pretty much on an ad hoc basis. Later, this crisis desk was disbanded. Did you have any involvement in either the establishment or disbanding of it, or any comment about it?*
MR. KENNAN: No, I didn't, and I know nothing about it really. I, fortunately, wasn't involved in any such crises.

MR. MORRISSEY: *Out of curiosity, since your academic affiliation is with Princeton, did John Kennedy ever remark to you on the fact that he once chose to attend this university?*
MR. KENNAN: He never did. I saw references to it in Princeton publications here and pictures of him as an undergraduate, but he never mentioned it to me. As a matter of fact, we never discussed anything personal. We didn't know each other that well, and we met in circumstances where he was too busy, I think, to permit himself any such luxury. I was awfully sorry that I hadn't had an opportunity to know him better personally, but I had a feeling that wouldn't really have been so easy.

MR. FISCHER: *Yes. I was going to remark: I appreciate the brilliance and precision of his mind and the beautiful style, the beautiful figure and his great achievements as President, but I have the impression that he was cold. I wonder whether you have. I never saw him.*
MR. KENNAN: Louis, not exactly cold. I didn't feel this. I felt that he had a certain real warmth, but that he was, in a sense, shy and somewhat set apart by his family background in the way that members of large and very solid

families sometimes are. In other words, a man who has had such an over-powering family intimacy, as I felt he had had, I think often finds that almost enough in life, and it is not so easy for him to seek real friendships outside of this. This was my feeling: that no outsider like myself could ever enter into his intimate circle at this stage of his life.

MR. FISCHER: *Robert Kennedy was a member of the same large family. He's the only Kennedy I've talked with. I had a forty-minute talk with him in March 1964. I felt he was warm and outgoing. We talked about John Kennedy; we talked about Robert's children. I've had letters from him. There was a warmth that emanated from him which I suspect did not emanate from John F. Kennedy. It's only a suspicion because I didn't know John F. Kennedy.*
MR. KENNAN: Well, I didn't have the impression of a cold person, but I had the impression of a person who guarded his inner self quite tightly from re-vealing. He had, of course, the sort of politician-actor's countenance. What Freud called the "persona," as distinct from the ego, that is, the outer personal-ity, was very highly developed with him. As in the case of most people who are on the political stage, he was acting his part in a way most of the time. But he always treated me, and others that I could see in his presence, kindly—in a kindly fashion—and not really cold. One didn't have the feeling that there was any underlying contempt or callousness or cruelty.

MR. FISCHER: *Oh no, no, no. But he didn't let down his hair, so to speak.*
MR. KENNAN: Certainly not in the personal sense. He didn't establish this kind of a personal bond. Mr. Truman was a more personal President than Jack Kennedy.

MR. FISCHER: *Yes. And Eisenhower? You had no sympathy, I suppose.*
MR. KENNAN: Well, Eisenhower, of course, was charming and disarming. You came away feeling frustrated (I always did, at any rate) from encounters with Ike. He was a good talker and much more intelligent than he was given credit for being. In the presence of his Cabinet, when he spoke, in my opinion he was head and shoulders above all of them except Foster [John Foster Dulles], and fully on a par with Foster in his understanding of foreign affairs. He was very good, but he, too, put you off with charm. I mean, in a way it was harder even to get nearer to Ike. You see, with Ike good fellowship was there to be had for the asking. I mean, if you'd offer to go out and play golf and so forth, you could have gone out. But how close you would really have gotten, I don't

know; because Ike had all the characteristic charm and evasiveness of royalty. It was just like talking with Queen Elizabeth. I mean, you came in, and you were well treated; he said interesting things; you went out, and you had beaten your head against a pillow. It wasn't this way with Jack Kennedy because he, of course, questioned you and listened very, very carefully to what you had to say and didn't put you off this way. On the other hand, this was impersonal in the sense that the subject matter was always confined to official life. Mind you, I'm sure he was kindly and nice and considerate of people, and, had I appealed to him in any personal situation, I'm sure that he would have responded. I, of course, never did that. He had his burdens.

MR. MORRISSEY: *Do you have any more questions? I don't either. I think we can stop there. Thank you very much.*

A Transcript of a Recorded Interview with George F. Kennan

Richard D. Challener / 1967

From the John Foster Dulles Oral History,
Princeton University Library. Copyright ©
George F. Kennan. Reprinted by permission.

CHALLENER: *I think you were going to begin by telling me when you began to have any significant contacts with Mr. Dulles.*

KENNAN: Yes. I cannot remember when I first met him. I may have met him socially before 1949. The first time I recall meeting him is when he came to the Department of State to work on the problem of the Japanese Peace Treaty, and this, I believe, was at some time in 1949.

I have notes in my diary of having attended the meetings of the committee which was chaired by Phil Jessup to study our policies with relation to the Far East. I have a note of attending a meeting of that committee on August 30, 1949. I said in my diary:

We spoke particularly of Southeast Asia and Japan. It is ironic that our principal reason for wanting a treaty of peace with Japan at this time is that it appears to be the only way of solving internal administrative difficulties with our own government.

Now, I think it possible that Mr. Dulles attended one or another of those meetings and that may have been the first time I met him.

I find another diary notation under the date of September 28th, 1949, to the effect that the members of the Policy Planning Staff met that morning with members of the Far Eastern Office and discussed the problems relating to the Japanese Peace Treaty. I cannot remember whether Mr. Dulles was present on that occasion. I doubt that he was, but it is my impression that he was already concerned at that time with the Peace Treaty problem.

On January 10, 1950, I find an entry that apparently refers to Mr. Dulles. It concerned my own plans for leaving government and entering academic life. I lunched that day with Mr. Dollard of the Carnegie Foundation and talked with him about the problem of my own future. I told him of my thought of going to the Institute for Advanced Study. He advised me—according to this diary note—not to accept "Dulles' suggestion of working for the Council." That was I suppose the Council on Foreign Relations, and the suggestion might have been made by Foster or by his brother, Allen. I cannot remember which it was who made it. Probably Allen, but possibly Foster.

In the notes for June 30, I find a reference to the fact that while I and others—namely, Messrs [Averell] Harriman and [Dean] Rusk—were talking with the Secretary of State, Mr. Dulles joined the group, and the discussion was broken off because there were things the Secretary wanted to discuss with Mr. Dulles. I don't know what they were. I left the room then.

Then, the following day, July 1st, 1950, we were joined at the intelligence briefings in the Secretary's office that morning by Mr. Dulles and the Secretary of the Army, Mr. Pace, and they participated in the discussion. I have a record of Mr. Pace's remarks, but I have nothing about what Mr. Dulles said.

On July 13, 1950, at the Secretary's morning meeting Mr. Dulles was present, as was I.

. . . A discussion ensued on the question of our general state of military unpreparedness and on the need for immediate measures to correct that situation. The Secretary raised a question as to just what measures of improvement we ought to recommend to the President and the national military establishment. Should we, for example, recommend there be full wartime mobilization?

Speaking to this point, I said that I did not think it a function of the State Department to define the actual measures which should be taken, but it should be sufficient for us to point out that the world situation called for a drastic improvement in the ability of this government to meet its international commitments, leaving it to others to define the measures to be taken in the internal field to achieve this end. . . .

The diary note continues as follows:

General Dean also emphasized that there was so much to be done that the important thing today was to make a beginning. There was no reason to delay the beginning until we could reach agreement as to the limit of our actions, and every reason not to delay it.

Mr. Dulles, when asked for his views on the situation, countered with this question: If we recognized a general war as one of the possibilities inherent in the situation, how did we envisage that such a war might begin? If there were isolated Soviet actions at different places around the periphery of Soviet power—as, for example, in Greece, Turkey, Iran, Indochina, Formosa, etc.—was it our view that we would continue to accept the responsibility for countering these situations by the use of United States armed force on limited theaters of operation? If not, at what point would we consider that these Soviet encroachments constitute a situation answerable only by general war, and how would we envisage them in the course of developments?

In my notes I added that I thought Mr. Dulles' question was a well-founded one, and one which should be taken into consideration in connection with each individual situation.

Next item: these are diary notes from July 17, 1950, and I shall read them verbatim because they concern Mr. Dulles' views, as well as my own.

. . . I then went to a big meeting in Rusk's office where they were discussing the question of a reply to [Jawaharlal] Nehru's mediation attempt. We had before us the text of Stalin's reply as received from the Indian government. It was typically Stalin: terse, extremely carefully worded, and pregnant with innuendo. It read as follows:

> I welcome your peaceable initiative. I fully share your point of view as re-
> gards the expediency of a peaceful regulation of the Korean question through
> the Security Council with the obligatory participation of representatives of the
> five great powers, including the Peoples Government of China. I believe that
> for a speedy settlement of the Korean question it would be expedient to hear in
> the Security Council representatives of the Korean people.

This made it clear that Stalin had no intention at present of concluding any deal about Korea, except on his own terms. And, indeed, why should he, as long as we were coming out worse in military operations? On the other hand, it indicated, as Chip [Bohlen] pointed out, that he probably had no intention of launching any direct aggressive move with Soviet forces further afield. Plainly he had chosen a spot where there was a maximum disagreement in the non-Communist camp—namely, the question of the Chinese Communist entry into the United Nations as a place for driving a wedge between his adversaries with the hope of causing a split between them which would carry over into the Korean question.

In the ensuing discussion, I suggested that we might side-step this one by stating that the question of the Chinese Communist entry into the United Nations was a separate one; and if anyone thought that we had any ulterior motives about that, we would be prepared to abstain in any vote on the admission of the Chinese Communists and to leave the question entirely to the judgment of the international community. It was my thought that in this way we might get this question removed from the area of discussion, so that Stalin could no longer exploit it as an excuse for not facing up to the situation in Korea. As far as I can see, it makes not the slightest difference whether or not the Chinese Communists come into the UN, and the fact that they might come in would be no reason, in my opinion, why we should feel obliged to have diplomatic relations with them. I hate to see what seems to me a minor issue, on which we never should have allowed ourselves to get hooked, become something which the Russians can use to our disadvantage in the Korean affair.

I was shouted down on this. Mr. Dulles pointed out that, if we were to do this, it would look as though we were retreating on the Chinese Communist issue in the belief that we were thereby buying some Russian concession about Korea, that this would not be the case and the Russians would still not agree to anything satisfactory about Korea, and that it would therefore look to our public as though we had been tricked into giving up something for nothing.

I recognized the force of this and realized that nothing can be done. But I hope that someday history will record this as an instance of the damage done to the conduct of our foreign policy by the irresponsible and bigoted interference of the China lobby and its friends in Congress.

I had a long talk with John Foster Dulles this afternoon. He was preparing a memorandum urging that we give immediate attention to the rearmament of Germany and Japan. I pointed out to him what I felt to be the significance of police forces as a means of bridging the gap between our need for creating strength in those quarters, on the one hand, and the fears of our allies, on the other.

I might just say, by way of elucidation of this last observation, that I had taken the position, ever since I was sent to Japan by General [George] Marshall in the spring of 1948 to discuss these matters with General [Douglas] MacArthur, that it would be better for us not to leave American forces in Japan and not to rearm the Japanese with conventional forces, but to give them a strong, smart, alert, well-armed military police force which could cope with any attempts at infiltration from the mainland and to let it go at that. I felt, in other words, that we should regard whatever danger there was to Japan from the Communist side as a political danger primarily and limit the Japanese defense really to the internal political security of the Japanese islands including their protection against infiltration from the mainland. And it was this view that I expressed generally in the governmental discussions of those years and expressed on this occasion to Mr. Dulles.

CHALLENER: *But Mr. Dulles believed in the actual rearmament of Japan?*
KENNAN: He did. He wanted to rearm both Germany and Japan. And I disagreed with him on this.

Now, you will note that the date of that was Monday, July 17. It had a repercussion very shortly thereafter. Before I come to that, however, I might just note that on the following day, Tuesday, July 18, and again I quote the diary:

. . . I wrote a memorandum to Rusk about the Japanese police problem, pleading again for action by the Department directed to the early establishment of a real central Japanese police force with a strong maritime branch which would constitute in effect a small navy capable of contributing significantly to Japanese defense against infiltration or landing of Communist agents or forces.

CHALLENER: *And this memorandum unquestionably went to Mr. Dulles?*
KENNAN: It certainly did. It must have been written with our conversation of the preceding day in mind and obviously it would have been sent to him. It was probably written, actually, as an effort on my part to oppose his desires to base the defense on Japan on regular conventional armed forces and on the indefinite retention of American garrisons in Japan, which I also did not approve of.

On July 19, 1950, according to the diary, I wrote another memorandum designed, as I expressed it, "to expedite action on the Japanese Peace Treaty." The diary note continues as follows:

. . . I have the feeling that, unless we move rapidly and intelligently in this matter, others may anticipate us with results which could be quite disastrous. Our failure to act in recent months has rested on disagreements between the State Department and the Defense establishment and on the lack of any incisive leadership or decision from any other quarter. We now have General MacArthur's views brought home by Mr. Dulles, and I see no excuse for our not doing everything possible within our competence to bring about rapid and courageous action.

I ought, perhaps, to note next, by way of explanation for what is about to come, that on July 21, at the Secretary's morning meeting, which I believe was probably attended by Mr. Dulles, I brought up the question of our failure to make it entirely clear that we were going to stop our military advance at the 38th parallel in Korea. The diary note goes as follows:

. . . I said that we must remember that what we were doing in Korea was, although for good political reasons, nevertheless, an unsound thing [and by that I meant in a military sense] and that the further we were to advance up the peninsula, the more unsound it would become from the military standpoint. If we were actually to advance beyond the neck of the peninsula, we would be getting into an area where mass could be used against us and where we would be distinctly at a disadvantage.

Similarly, on July 25, there was a meeting at the consultants' level of the National Security Council at which I spoke at length on the problem of Communist China. I mention that only because at some point here I attended a meeting having to do with Far Eastern affairs which was also attended by Mr. Dulles. I can't remember exactly whether it was on that occasion or some other, but it was, in any case, on an occasion that I expressed my own view that we needn't be afraid of letting the Chinese Communists be admitted to the United Nations if the others wanted to have them. I did not—all the way through here—advocate that we, ourselves, should propose them or should even vote for them. I was saying that I saw no reason why we should oppose a majority feeling in the UN that they ought to be there.

I find on looking further through the diary, that the meeting in question was one which took place on July 28, and it was, indeed, attended by Mr. Dulles. I stated at length my views ending with the following passages, which will give an idea of the tenor of this discussion.

. . . My proposal was that we state frankly that in our opinion the Peking regime had not shown a due sense of responsibility for its international obligations; that its international behavior had been offensive and childish and even such as to throw doubt on its independence of action in the international field; that we, for these reasons, had not recognized it and saw no reason to do so on the basis of its behavior to date; that since, however, our motives in this question and this matter had been widely questioned, and since it had been alleged that we had ulterior purposes in the position we had taken on this subject, we were prepared, as a pledge of the integrity of our position, to abstain completely from all further participation in the discussion or the consideration of this problem in the United Nations bodies, from any voting on the subject, and from any sort of pressure or intervention with any other power concerning the way in which it should vote. It was our hope that each country would vote on this question as it thought best in the light of careful consideration of what was involved, and we were prepared to abide entirely by the results of such a decision. . . .

Then the diary note continues as follows:

. . . This view was rejected by Bohlen and Dulles primarily on the ground that it would confuse American public opinion and weaken support for the President's program looking toward the strengthening of our defenses, and this view was eventually upheld by the Secretary.

I said that I could very well understand this, but I shuddered over the implications of it, for it implied that we could not adopt an adequate defense position without working our people up into an emotional state and that this emotional state, rather than a cool and unemotional appraisal of national interest, would then have to be the determinant of our action. The position we were taking seemed to me to imply acceptance of the theory that in the last analysis the UN would not be universal, but would be an Article 51 alliance against Russia. It seemed further to imply that the basis of our policy in the Far East from here on out would be an emotional anti-Communism which would ignore the value to ourselves of a possible balance between the existing forces on the Asiatic continent, would force everyone (including Chiang Kai-shek) to declare himself either for us or against us; that this would break the unity, not only of the non-Communist countries of Asia, but also of the non-Communist community in general, and would be beyond our military capacity to support. It rested, I said, on the encouragement in the minds of our people of a false belief that we were a strong power in Asia, whereas we are in reality a weak one. Only the very strong can take high and mighty moral positions and ignore the possibilities of balance among the opposing forces. The weak must accept realities and exploit those realities to their advantage as best they can.

With Bohlen and Dulles, as I say, the objections were laid to public opinion. With Rusk and some of the others, I think there was a real sense of moral indignation about the Chinese Communists.

Now, that was, I repeat on Friday, July 28th. On Monday, July 31, after the weekend (and again I quote the diary) . . .

. . . A member of the Planning Staff dropped in to tell me that he had learned from one journalist, who had learned it from another journalist, that Mr. Dulles had said to journalist number two that, while he used to think highly of George Kennan, he had now concluded that he was a very dangerous man, that he was advocating the admission of the Chinese Communists to the United Nations and a cessation of the United States military action at the 38th parallel. This information had been passed along to the member of the Planning Staff under such solemn vows of secrecy and discretion that I saw nothing I could do about it, but it seemed to me to raise serious problems about the privacy of discussion among top officials in the Department in the presence of the policy adviser from the Republican Party.

This was the Secretary's morning meeting and was regarded as absolutely top secret in the Department. I never would have said these things if I'd had the faintest idea that this was going to the press. These were internal discussions with the Department of State in which I thought, also, that anyone was at liberty in discussing problems on which no decision had yet been taken to discuss them freely and to put forward any sort of idea that commended itself to him for discussion. And the idea that one should run off—taking opinions that have been stated in a preliminary discussion of this nature—and expose them to the press as evidence of the iniquity of one of your colleagues was to me, I must say, highly shocking.

I come now to an item in the diary from Monday, August 21, 1950:

> A few days ago I received from Mr. Dulles a text of the short draft he had made for a Japanese Peace Treaty. The brevity of the draft was the result of my own urgings, and in this respect it was an attempt to meet my aversion to a long and legalistic document. Being pressed with many other things, and not feeling that my responsibility was directly involved, I did not comment on it.
>
> Another document, which came to my attention in the past few days was a report from our diplomatic mission in Tokyo—a carefully drafted and thoughtful analytical study of the Japanese Peace Treaty question with particular emphasis on probable Japanese reactions to the various possibilities. The mission warned against any attempt to station troops in Japan in the post-Treaty period except on the basis of a voluntary request of the Japanese government or as part of some international guarantee of Japan.
>
> Today I received from Mr. Dulles a brief memo putting me on the spot by saying that, if he did not hear further from me in this matter, he would interpret my silence as approval of the draft he had sent to me. I did not feel at liberty to discuss frankly with him all of my views about the Japanese Peace Treaty question in its relation to the wider problems of Far Eastern policy, for I was afraid that they might appear to be in opposition to some of those stated by the President or the Secretary and that I would give the impression, just as I was leaving the Department, that my departure had something to do with differences of opinion about policy matters. I therefore gave Mr. Dulles only a conditional reply based on the assumption that the decision to leave forces in Japan had already been taken and was, therefore, not open to discussion. But since I realized that I had never really tried to express my views succinctly, even for the Secretary, on this broader subject, I sat down and wrote a memorandum for him.

This completes, so far as I can recall, the dealings that I had with Mr. Dulles during the period when I was serving in the State Department as Director of the Policy Planning Staff and Counselor of the Department and when he was involved in Departmental affairs through his work on the Japanese Peace Treaty.

The next contacts that I recall having with Mr. Dulles were in the autumn of 1952. I had been serving throughout most of that year as Ambassador to Moscow. But at the end of September, or the beginning of October, I was declared persona non grata by the Soviet government.

The Truman administration—for reasons that I have never understood—got the idea that it might be unwise to let me come home before the elections, that this might get into the election campaign in some way or other, and I was therefore left to stay in Bad Godesberg at our mission to the West German government until the election had taken place.

On October 2nd, Mr. Dulles sent me a note—a copy of which I do not appear to have—enclosing the text of a speech that he had recently given before the Missouri Bar Association. I acknowledged it on October 22—I imagine that it had followed me to Moscow and thence to Bonn—thanking him for it and saying:

. . . I am enclosing a copy of some observations which I recently drew up for another purpose, but which bear on the point you make. They will give you a somewhat clearer idea of how I feel about morality in foreign policy.

I will ask you, if you will, to keep them closely and to see that they do not by any chance get into the public prints, because I don't feel that I want to make any public statements on this subject at the present time.

With all good wishes,

Sincerely yours . . . .

Mr. Dulles acknowledged that note from his New York, 91st Street, office on October 29th as follows:

Dear George:

I have your letter of October 22nd. I read the enclosure with much interest. I find it clarifying, although I do believe that there are certain basic moral concepts which all peoples and nations can and do comprehend and to which it is legitimate to appeal as providing some common standard of international conduct. Our common law came out of this conception, and I would hope in due course there would develop some sort of international common law.

Allen got back yesterday and told me that he had had a good talk with you in Germany.

I will, of course, treat your enclosure as strictly confidential. . . .

I arrived back in this country on November 11, 1952. The change of administration, of course, had not yet taken place. And the Truman administration saw—for obvious reasons—no point in making another appointment of an Ambassador to Moscow in the last weeks of its incumbency. Not knowing what else to do, and nobody in the Department being in any way concerned, I therefore went with my family to my home in Pennsylvania and lived there from that time on.

During the month of December I read a good deal of gossip in the public prints concerning the prospective appointments of the Eisenhower administration, but I did not think that it would be either tactful or helpful of me to inquire what plans they had for me or for the ambassadorship to Moscow, so I made no such inquiries. I was still technically at that time the Ambassador to the Soviet Union, although not persona grata to the Soviet government. I did rather think that I would hear something from the new administration about my next appointment at some time before they took office—which, as I recall it, was the 20th of January.

CHALLENER: *That's right.*
KENNAN: But I heard not a single word. I assumed that it would be offered another appointment because I was a career Foreign Service officer of about twenty-five years standing, at that time; and while the fact that the Soviet government had declared me persona non grata was an unpleasant episode in my career and might have reflected unfavorably upon me, as well as upon the Soviet government, nevertheless, I did not suppose that it would be held against me to such an extent as to invalidate me from any usefulness in future service. So, I was a little surprised not to hear anything from the new administration before they took over as to what they proposed to do with me.

Meanwhile, I was invited by the Pennsylvania Bar Association to speak to their annual meeting—which was to be held, I believe, at Scranton on January 16. I accepted this. This was one of the most important bar associations in the country. I prepared a speech on the subject of Soviet-American relations, which was the only public statement of this sort I ever made during the period of my incumbency as Ambassador. I cleared it with the Department of State, which was the proper thing to do and the only thing I could do, and I delivered it then as per schedule on the 16th.

I might read into the record here the document in which I wrote this all up at the time. It was written, actually, on March 13, 1953.

At the time of the election I had had no communication with anyone in the new administration concerning my own personal position. I arrived home November 11, 1952, one week after the election. I was in Washington that week and again the following week at which time I paid my respects to the Secretary of State, Mr. Acheson. Later in the month, after President Truman's return from an absence to Washington, I came to Washington again and called on him. Naturally, in view of their impending departure from office, neither President Truman nor Secretary Acheson discussed with me the question of my future service with the government.

Having known both General Eisenhower and Mr. John Foster Dulles personally, I expected to be approached at some point before the new administration took office and to have an opportunity to give them my views, not only concerning the state of US-Soviet relations, but also concerning the future of the Moscow Embassy and the disposition that was to be made of myself under the new administration. However, the weeks passed and nothing was said to me.

Early in December, as I recall, I met Mr. Allen Dulles at a friend's home and talked with him for a few minutes. He asked me what I had thought of with respect to my own future. I said I could tell him first what I did not want, which was to be kept around Washington as an adviser without power—just far enough from the administration so that my advice could be ignored with impunity and near enough to it so that it would be inhibited from public discussion of any policy questions. Rather than that, I said, I would prefer another mission in the field and did not feel that it ought to be necessarily one of the big embassies.

In making these observations to Mr. Allen Dulles, I was still proceeding on the assumption that the attitude of the new administration toward me was a friendly and respectful one and that, even though they might not feel that they could use me in a high position, they would still attach value to my opinions and to the preservation of a mutual relationship of cordiality and understanding. As the weeks passed, however, after this conversation and still no word was forthcoming from any responsible person in the new administration, I began to realize that this assumption was not fully grounded and that the President and John Foster Dulles were apparently not interested either in discussing with me my future or that of the Moscow position, nor were they interested in my views about the Soviet Union or the U.S.-Soviet relations.

In view of the position I had just occupied in Moscow, the experience I had previously had in Soviet affairs, and the extent to which my name was publicly associated with problems of Soviet-American relations, I could not help but view this as a very serious and disturbing situation. I was worried, furthermore, about my duties to the many people outside the government who had given me their confidence and encouragement in the past and who, I knew, would wish to have some indication from me as to my feelings about Soviet-American relations after the Moscow experience. I had returned from Moscow deeply preoccupied with these problems, to which I had been exposed probably as intensively and painfully as any other American. The outgoing administration had shown no serious interest in my views on these subjects, but this was natural, since there was nothing more they could do, and they were all tired and in the throes of departure. But if the new administration were also to be uninterested, and if I were to say nothing to the public, it would mean that my feelings on this subject, whatever they were worth, would remain wholly unexpressed and would be of no use to anyone anywhere.

For approximately a year since I had first been told of the intention to appoint me as the Ambassador to Moscow, I had remained silent and had given no personal statements about Soviet-American relations. In view of this significant silence in the new administration, it was clear that, if I waited until they took office, I would not be able to speak at all on this subject, since I could not speak for them and yet could not talk about these matters publicly without consultation with them. It seemed to me, therefore, that any statement I might make on this subject should be made during the incumbency of the old administration in order that the new one might remain wholly uncommitted by what I said.

I therefore accepted the invitation of the Pennsylvania State Bar Association to address its annual meeting at Scranton on January 16 and addressed my remarks on that occasion to the subject of Soviet-American relations. I did this with specific regard to the fact that the incoming administration had made no attempt to get in touch with me on those questions. Had I been given any reason to suppose that the new administration intended to use my views on this subject and had I been in any sort of communication with them, I would have been happy to submit the speech to Mr. Dulles, as well as to Mr. Acheson, for clearance and to adjust to his requirements. But since he made no effort to communicate with me about these matters, I saw no reason to do so and feared (quite correctly as it turned out) that unless I stated my views at that time, I would have no further opportunity to do so in the coming period.

The Scranton speech was duly cleared with the existing Truman administration before delivery. It was scarcely reported in the New York press at the time of delivery. The *New York Times* carried only a brief reference to it on an inside page in one of its editions the following day. The *Herald Tribune* had nothing at all. However, Ferdinand Kuhn, of the *Washington Post*, wrote a story which was carried on the front page calling attention to the passage about interference in the internal affairs of other governments and playing this up as intended to be critical of the views of Mr. Dulles.

This seemed to me to be very overdrawn, since Mr. Dulles had spoken only of moral suasion, whereas I had spoken of direct interference by one government in the internal affairs of another country. I had not mentioned Mr. Dulles or the new administration in any way, and the passage was not given any tinge of controversial tone. I felt rather badly that a speech which was not recorded in its entirety by a single organ of the daily press was being played up in this way.

I arrived in Washington on the evening of the day following the speech, January 17th, and the following morning, Sunday, January 18th, I handed to Mr. Freeman Matthews . . .

(I should interpolate that he was, I think, then at the head of the European Office at the Department of State.)

. . . the following memorandum:

Washington
January 18, 1953

Dear Doc:

On arriving in Washington yesterday evening I was amazed and shocked to see what the Washington papers had done with the remarks I made before the Pennsylvania Bar Association on Friday evening, and while I think this was largely a one-day sensation and restricted to the Washington itself (the New York papers had nothing about it), there are one or two things about it which I think Mr. Dulles ought to know.

I am leaving for my home in the country and will not be on hand here for the next few days. Furthermore, I do not know where Mr. Dulles is and doubt that he would wish to be bothered about it directly by me in these coming days; so I am writing this to you in order that you may be informed and able to give explanations if they are asked.

The points I wish to make are these:

(1) The speech was intended as the first, last, and only major statement made by myself on Soviet-American relations during the period of my incumbency as Ambassador to the USSR.

(2) It was written and distributed to the press before I knew anything of Mr. Dulles' statement before the Foreign Relations Committee.

(3) From what I knew of Mr. Dulles' views on this subject, which was only what I had seen in the press, I did not have the impression that there was any important difference between us. The remarks did not have him in mind, but other certain editors, legislators, and professional propagandists for minority groups interested in Russia who would like to see us commit ourselves to a policy of intervention.

(4) I deliberately chose a time prior to the inauguration to make this statement in order that there could be no question of any responsibility of the new administration for the views expressed.

I conclude that this will create a problem with regard to my future assignment. I think, therefore, that Mr. Dulles might wish to know the following:

If I read correctly the legislation, I am eligible for retirement when I reach the age of fifty, which will be a little more than a year from now—February 16, 1954. My only desire or ambition with regard to government service is to make myself useful in some capacity until I become eligible for retirement and then to retire to private life. I am not eager for any post of senior responsibility in this intervening period and would be perfectly happy to take the sort of job that would normally be given to a Foreign Service officer of my rank and experience. I will be glad to try to make all this plain to outsiders if that would be of help to any one.

Finally, if the Department thinks it would be helpful, I would be glad to have the following statement or one along these lines released to the press tomorrow as coming from me:

> I have noted with surprise and regret the interpretation placed by part of the press on the remarks I recently made before the Pennsylvania State Bar Association: namely, that they were intended to be critical of the views previously expressed by Mr. Dulles. I was not aware that there was any important difference between his views and mine on the subject in question and find it difficult to understand how such an interpretation could be arrived at.

In case such a statement should be issued, I would appreciate it that the press might be told that this was the only statement I expect to make on the matter, and that I shall not be able to amplify it or comment on it in any way.

I should add that at that time I did not know for sure that it was technically possible for me to retire in the coming spring, and I was going on the assumption that I would have to serve for at least another year. I still had not realized how strong were Mr. Dulles' negative feelings with regard to myself.

I returned to Washington on January 22nd and 23rd. By this time the new administration had taken over. On the second of those days Mr. Dulles asked to see me in the presence of Mr. [Carl] McCardle to examine what could be done to stop the undesirable press attention to this alleged controversy, since a number of papers and commentators were continuing to play it up as a major quarrel between the two of us.

I told him what I meant by the passage in question. He talked about his views on this subject for four or five minutes and then told McCardle and me to work out some statement for the press. The result was the following statement issued by Mr. McDermott the same afternoon:

> With regard to press discussion of his recent speech at Scranton, this speech was prepared by Mr. Kennan, cleared in the normal fashion in the Department of State, distributed to the press before Mr. Dulles' appearance before the Senate Foreign Relations Committee, and had no relation to Mr. Dulles' remarks. Mr. Kennan has conferred with the Secretary about this matter. Mr. Dulles wishes it to be known that he considers the episode closed.

After this incident the silence of the new administration with respect to myself was resumed. Stories appeared from time to time in the press about assignments which were allegedly given to me. At one time it was Cairo. At another time, approximately

February 6th, the *New York Times* came out with a front page story listing a number of appointments the new administration expected to make, including myself as Minister to Switzerland. Later it was said that I would be appointed to Yugoslavia. However, throughout all this period, I received no communication whatsoever from the administration.

While I learned privately of the plans to appoint Bohlen as my successor in Moscow, nothing was officially communicated to me about this, and I was not even apprised of the approach made to the Soviet government concerning the agrément for him. The submission of his name to the Senate as my successor did seem to me, however, to create a situation which called for some sort of discussion of my position with the new administration. I therefore went to Mr. Lourie, Under Secretary of State, on February 25, and left him with the following memorandum:

> I have refrained until this time from taking up with Mr. Dulles or the President the question of what I am to do in the future because I knew that they had many preoccupations in these early weeks of President Eisenhower's incumbency, and I did not want to press them unnecessarily. However, Mr. Bohlen's appointment as my successor has now been announced, and I must assume that within a short time the President will accept my letter of resignation, which he has had before him since he assumed office.
>
> It is my understanding that if, after laying down my present position as Ambassador to the Soviet Union, I receive no new appointment within three months, I will automatically be retired with full retirement benefits. I am writing this to say that unless the President has for me some work of real importance for which he particularly wants my services, I would be prepared to retire this spring in the manner mentioned above. For various family reasons it is necessary for me to make some sort of plans for the coming period. Unless I am informed to the contrary, I shall go ahead and make my plans on the assumption that the administration is prepared to permit me to retire at the completion of the three-months period.
>
> While I shall do my best to discourage press speculation about my future at this time, many prominent journalists are already curious about it, and Mr. Bohlen's appointment is bound to cause them to ask questions. I think it unavoidable, in any case, that my retirement at this time will lead to a certain amount of comment and criticism, but this may be worse the longer a decision is postponed and for this reason the administration will wish to give attention at an early date to the public relations aspect of this matter.

Despite the fact that this memorandum specifically called attention to the need for an early consideration of the public relations aspect of this matter, I received no reply to it in the ensuing days, nor any communication concerning my future status.

The memorandum from which I have been reading then goes ahead to tell of two or three requests that I got in the ensuing days to give advice to the government at lower echelons. I was asked by my friend, Chip Bohlen, to come to Washington to advise concerning the questions arising from Stalin's death. Mr. C. D. Jackson asked me to come down to advise on matters with which he was connected. Dr. Raymond Sontag of the CIA called to ask me to continue to function as an adviser to that organization.

I resume, then, the reading from the memorandum:

. . . Confronted with these new demands that I give advice to the government at lower echelons, I thought I had better ask for some official clarification of my status in this respect and also to repeat my request for some information about my future. I therefore sent to Mr. Lourie for transmission to the Secretary and the President the following memorandum on March 10:

> Mr. Lourie has no doubt shown you the memorandum I addressed to him on February 25. In that memorandum I stated that I would be prepared to retire this spring unless the President has some work of real importance for which he particularly wants my services. I have still had no word of any sort from you or the President as to your views about my future, and I would be grateful for some indication of the views of the President and yourself on the question.
>
> Meanwhile, pending some decision as to my future assignment, I am troubled to know what response to give to numerous requests that I give advice to various officers of the government. During the past few days I have been approached by Mr. C. D. Jackson, by Mr. William Jackson's committee, by Mr. Allen Dulles, and by other echelons of the Central Intelligence Agency with a request to assist them with advice of one sort or another. I have agreed to see Mr. C. D. Jackson this afternoon, and I shall do so, but I question whether I should accept any further requests of this sort unless I have some grounds to feel that it is the desire of the President and yourself that I do so.
>
> Since a period of more than three months must elapse before I can retire, I assume this question will arise repeatedly, and I would appreciate your instructions.

At two-thirty on the afternoon of March 10, I called on Mr. C. D. Jackson who told me of certain problems with which he was concerned and asked my advice. I pointed out to him that my status under the new administration was entirely unclarified, that I had seen no official papers to speak of for a period of five months, that I therefore had knowledge of the present state of affairs largely from the newspapers, that I had no opportunity to be instructed in the thoughts or policies of the new administration, that I could not speak with any rank in the Department of State, and that therefore I felt inhibited in giving him any advice.

He said he realized all of this, but he would nevertheless like to get simply my reaction as an individual to certain of the ideas he had advanced. On this basis I gave him my reaction.

Before I left he said he was sure there was some misunderstanding about my position in the government. He could not believe that the President had meant to convey to me the impression I had received. He would speak with Mr. Dulles about it to see whether the matter could not be clarified.

I returned to the farm that afternoon. The following afternoon I received another message from Jackson's office to the effect that he would have something toward the end of the week that he would want to show me. I therefore came down to Washington again on Thursday, March 12, and arranged to call on Mr. Jackson the following morning.

That afternoon I received a call from Mr. William Lawrence of the *New York Times* who said that he had heard that I was to be retired and wanted to know whether I could confirm that. I told him I had received no communication of any sort from the new administration with regard to my status. The following Monday, March 13, the *New York Times* carried a front page story by Mr. Lawrence to the effect that he had learned from high administration sources that I was to be retired in the near future.

Shortly after I had reached the office I received a phone call from Mr. [Frank] Wisner in CIA who said that he was authorized by Mr. Allen Dulles to tell me that Mr. Dulles would very much like to have me take Dr. Sontag's position, which he was going to leave in the near future, or any other high position in the CIA where my knowledge and experience could be utilized.

I saw Mr. Jackson again in the morning. He told me of the progress in the matters he had discussed with me two or three days before. I was able to be of little help to him.

I was disturbed on this same day to read in the papers of the continuing difficulties in obtaining confirmation in the Senate of Bohlen's appointment. I felt that this was really part of the same problem and that altogether these things were bound soon to come to some sort of climax.

On that same day, apparently, I was asked to come in and see the Secretary of State, Mr. Dulles, and did so. I have now only my own recollections to go on. He said to me—and these, I think, were his exact words—he knew of "no niche" for me in the Department or the Foreign Service.

I was taken aback by this statement, because it was an unusual one to be made to a Foreign Service officer of twenty-five years standing who was in good graces and who had not, at least, received any word of criticism from anyone of higher office. I was so taken aback that I just didn't react to it and said, "Very well."

Before I left, he said, "Now, I wish you'd sit down and tell me what you think about the state of affairs in Russia." I did talk a little bit about it. And his reaction to that was, "Well, now that really interests me. I hope you'll come back and see me occasionally. When you talk about these things, I really find it interesting, and there are not many people that interest me in this way."

I said, "What are we going to do about the announcement of my retirement?"

And he said, "Well, you'd better get together with my press secretary, Mr. McCardle. He will work out something."

So, I did get together with Mr. McCardle . . . Let me see—this must have been some time later. I probably consulted with McCardle after leaving the Secretary, and on March 16, we apparently agreed—McCardle and myself and the Secretary—that nothing would be announced for the moment about my retirement in view of the suggestion advanced by Mr. Allen Dulles that I accept service in the coming period with the Central Intelligence Agency.

Oh, now I recall what happened. After Mr. Dulles spoke to me on March 13, and told me that he had no place for me in the Service—I was then staying at Chip Bohlen's house, and I went directly from the Secretary's office back there to his house—I was amazed and immensely gratified to receive only a few minutes later a personal visit from Mr. Allen Dulles, who offered me a position with the Central Intelligence Agency. I wanted to consider this. And for this reason—apparently I talked again with the Secretary on March 16th—it was agreed that for the moment nothing would be announced about my retirement in view of Mr. Allen Dulles' suggestion.

CHALLENER: *This is Assistant Secretary McCardle.*
KENNAN: I had discussed it with him, but I also discussed it again on March 16th with the Secretary, himself.

CHALLENER: *I see. Yes.*
KENNAN: And we agreed that in view of Allen's offer nothing, for the moment, would be announced.

On March 20, I wrote to Mr. Foster Dulles from my home in Pennsylvania and said that much as I appreciated Allen Dulles' suggestion, "I have concluded that I would prefer not to remain in government service in any capacity at this time, but rather to retire as envisaged in our conversation on March 13. I am advising Mr. Allen Dulles accordingly."

I went on to say:

I do not feel that I am in a proper position to advise the Department as to the manner in which this ought to be announced and am quite content to leave this to your discretion. I do think, however, that something should be announced at the earliest convenient opportunity. I have fortunately not been queried by reporters on this subject since our recent conversation, but were I now to be so queried I would of course no longer be able to say that we have not communicated in the matter, and I should find myself embarrassed to attempt to conceal for long the nature of the arrangements arrived at.

As a result of this, I think, I came to Washington at some point in the next few days and met with Mr. McCardle who confessed to me that he did not feel himself up to the task of drafting a suitable communique, so I said, "Let me think over it while I have lunch," and I scratched something out at the table and brought it back to him, to which his reaction was, "Geez, Mr. Ambassador, that's elegant. I couldn't have written that!"

Well, anyway, the upshot of all this was that on April 6th Mr. Dulles wrote me the following letter:

Dear Mr. Kennan:

Last January you told me that you did not consider yourself available for reassignment in the Foreign Service and requested that you be permitted to retire as soon as the necessary arrangements could be made. You also indicated that you would be glad to continue to be available to the government as a consultant. No action was taken at that time on your proposed retirement, and I hoped that some mutually agreeable alternative could be arrived at, which would make more readily available to the government your special talents, particularly in relation with Russian matters.

I understand, however, that it is still your desire to receive no further assignment, but to be allowed to retire after the lapse of a further period of three months in accordance with the pertinent provisions of the law.

In view of your continuing desire in this respect, I feel that I have no alternative but to comply with your wishes. In doing so, I want to express the very high personal esteem in which I told you and to express the hope that you will, as you indicated in January, continue to be available to the government as a consultant. I have every expectation that not only in this Department, but other Departments of government may want to call upon you.

With good wishes and renewed thanks for the valued and patriotic contributions that you have made, I am,

Sincerely yours . . .

Now, I received that but was very unhappy about it, because it said, "Last January you told me that you did not consider yourself available for reassignment." I drew up on April 7, a long memorandum explaining what the real situation was and the reasons why I had offered to resign in January and objecting to this wording. I said:

I think a more accurate wording of the first sentence would be something like this: "You have indicated to me that you were not seeking reassignment in the Foreign Service and were prepared to retire as soon as the necessary arrangements could be made."

I cannot, however, remember what was done with that or whether the letter was ever corrected. I would have to search my own files to find out.

This was the end of it. The provision of the act under which I was permitted to retire was one which I believe had never been invoked before. It was put into the act to enable an administration—a President—to get rid of an incompetent Ambassador without embarrassment, and I was the first person to retire under it.

I was not, however, altogether unhappy, and this is one reason why I did not protest more than I did, because they had neglected to state in writing this provision that you had to be of retirement age. The result meant that I could retire—the only person who could—at the age of forty-nine on a pension for life. I had this assessed by a banking friend in New York who told me it was worth 133 thousand dollars on an actuarial basis. And I thought that balancing this off against the problematical prospects of serving under Mr. Dulles and Mr. Eisenhower that I would be just as well off outside.

This whole flap had its amusing aspects, because for one thing I was told privately—I don't know how true it is—that one reason that Mr. Dulles wanted to get rid of me was that he thought that any further assignment for me would run into difficulties with the Senate. I had been prominently involved, it is true, in defending certain of the victims of McCarthyism—quite a series of them, good friends of mine. And I was even subpoenaed in those weeks by the Internal Security Sub-committee of the Senate Committee of the Judiciary and very brutally questioned in a manner to indicate that they had suspicions of my own loyalty. And I heard it said that he had let me go because he didn't want to have any argument with the Senators about my confirmation.

CHALLENER: *By this time the Bohlen flap had already developed in the Senate.*

KENNAN: The Bohlen flap had already developed. But there was one thing that Mr. Dulles, I think, never knew—I never thought it my business to tell him, but it adds an amusing touch to it—that just in these weeks, while the Bohlen confirmation was boiling as a controversial subject on Capitol Hill, I received a phone call up in my home in Pennsylvania from Senator [Homer] Ferguson of Michigan, who asked me whether I would mind coming down to Washington to see him. I had never met him before, but I did make the trip down there and called on him. And he said, "Really, what I called you down here for, I just want to ask your opinion. Should we confirm this fellow Bohlen?"

And I said, "Of course, you should," and told him why, and went back to my farm.

This always amused me in connection with Mr. Dulles' suspicion that I, myself, would not have been confirmed.

The second aspect of this which probably ought to be in the record, too, is a rather amusing one. This is confidential and I assume that none of this will be released without my own approval.

CHALLENER: *That's right.*

KENNAN: Just as the three months were running out, and I was about to retire finally—maybe even after, for all I remember—I was asked to come down to Washington, this time by Bobby Cutler, the President's assistant. And Mr. Cutler told me that the President was going to set up a top secret and extremely important and elaborate project over the summer to evolve the main lines of his foreign policy toward the Communist bloc.

CHALLENER: *The Solarium Study.*

KENNAN: The Solarium Study. There were to be three teams, and I was asked whether I would head one of them. Well, I did, and we worked all summer in the privacy of the old National War College building, where I had functioned before as Deputy for Foreign Affairs. And at the end of this time, the three teams were brought to the White House and the Cabinet was assembled.

Each of the teams was asked to defend one of three possible policies towards the Communist bloc. I didn't like this procedure at all, because I hated to be made a priori the advocate of a given view on a side. But fortunately, of the three views in question the one that I was asked to defend was closest to my own. And I did defend it, and finally presented it, at the termination of the exercise, to the assembled Cabinet members, including Mr. Dulles. And when it was done, the President said that he thought our team had had the best of it and that what we had outlined should be the foreign policy of the administration presently in Washington. So, in a curious sense, at the same time that I was dropped from the government service, I was asked to write the ticket insofar as policy toward the Soviet Union was concerned. And this, of course, put me in mind again of Foster's statement, when he had dropped me, that he hoped I'd come back again and discuss it with him.

I think actually that one of his reasons for dropping me—well, he had several, probably—was that he thought there might be embarrassment before the Congress. Another was that he had been a little shocked by the views I had expressed about bringing Communist China into the UN and so forth—shocked not so much at that I should have thought these things, as that I should have been politically so inept as to expose such thoughts to others in Washington.

But, thirdly, I think he realized that in a sense there was a great intimacy of thought between himself and myself. That is, we differed on certain things, but in a way we were more deeply into this subject matter than any two people in Washington—we understood each other better. Because we had the same kind of mind in certain respects. He knew he was going to have to follow *in practice* the line I had laid down, and I think he didn't want me around Washington in any responsible capacity, because he didn't want it to be said that I was inspiring his ideas. He wanted to take full credit for everything that he did. And he didn't want anything said of the sort that was said with regard to the Marshall Plan—that I had suggested some of these things to General Marshall.

Of course, this, in itself, did not preclude his offering me a less important diplomatic assignment—which I would have taken at that time. So, I suppose that the question of Senatorial confirmation also came into it.

CHALLENER: *It gave them a book, probably, to hang their hat on.*
KENNAN: Yes. It may have been.

CHALLENER: *May I ask one question now?*
KENNAN: Yes.

CHALLENER: *I have heard the story from a Washington newspaperman that about this time you talked to a member of the British Foreign Service, Adam Watson . . .*

KENNAN: Yes, that's right.

CHALLENER: . . . *in which you indicated that John Foster Dulles had to get rid of you so that he could copy your policy.*
KENNAN: Well, there's something in it. It, perhaps, shouldn't be stated quite that way.

The fact of the matter is that, although we disagreed on what should be said publicly on such matters as liberation of the Eastern European countries, we did not disagree, really, on what should be done practically. Here, he really knew that he would have no choice but to follow my line. And I think that he just didn't want it to appear that he was in any form of partnership with me, because he knew that he would have to do things which would lend themselves to the interpretation of being things that had been part of my political philosophy.

CHALLENER: *Well, at that time did you think of him as a man who was committed to this kind of "roll back" and "liberation" cause or a man who might end up practising, in a sense, the more established position?*
KENNAN: I thought exactly that—that he would practice much the same as what we had been doing, which indeed he did, but that he was terribly concerned for his image, so to speak, vis a vis the Republican majority in the Senate, and he would go very far, indeed, to please these people by what he said.

CHALLENER: *Yes, publicly.*
KENNAN: And this is just exactly what he did.

CHALLENER: *Do you think this offer of the CIA was worked out between the two brothers?*
KENNAN: Quite frankly, I think that the brothers disagreed quite strongly over the question of dismissing me from government, and that Allen's visit to me—he left his office and came right over to the house where I was staying— was the most tactful and forceful way he could find of distancing himself from his brother's action. And the week after that, as I recall it, Mrs. Eleanor Dulles, whom neither my wife nor myself had ever met, called up and asked us to a very nice, quiet, intimate dinner at her home out in Virginia. It was a very pleasant evening, and this obviously, too, was a gesture.

I have the feeling that the family felt it to be quite a shabby thing—the way that this had happened and the way that I had been released—and had argued with him about it, and that both his brother and his sister went out of their way then to make it evident to Mrs. Kennan and myself, although quite properly and tactfully never saying so specifically, that they were not in agreement with what their brother had done. I appreciated this very deeply, and I've always been very grateful to them both ever since.

The only reason I didn't take the position with CIA was that I felt that if I wasn't wanted in the government in the place where I had been for twenty-five years, I would just rather not be in it anywhere. So, I didn't accept it. But I would have been happy, otherwise, to be associated with Allen.

CHALLENER: *His was probably the one agency of government, too, that resisted the McCarthyism.*
KENNAN: Yes. Well this was already a tremendously painful time. And I'll tell you another reason that I didn't mind leaving government so much, and that was the treatment of John (Paton) Davies.

CHALLENER: *Yes. I was going to ask you about that.*
KENNAN: You see, Davies was never found guilty in any of his hearings, but what he was accused of was something he had done as a member of my Planning Staff in the Department. And, while it was not anything that he had done under specific instructions from me, he had done it with my general confidence and authority to go ahead, behave maturely, and to advance ideas and to discuss it with other people in the government. And what happened there again was so shocking, as indeed was his final dismissal, that I think I probably would have had to resign over the Davies case had I not dropped out when I did. So, it's probably all for the best. And it was the beginning, for me, of an academic career which has been a very rich one, so I don't feel regret in that respect.

I could have wished for another way of leaving the Service. It was in all respects a very strange time. When the day finally came for me to leave Washington, I remember that there was only one person in the Department of State then that I could find to say good-by to, and that was the receptionist up on fifth floor—and this was after a quarter of a century in the Foreign Service. My retirement was, so far as I can recall, never mentioned by the *Foreign Service Journal*. I just got in a car and drove away. It was a strange way to finish a career.

CHALLENER: *Indeed, it would seem to be. May I probe back a little bit on the '49 to '52 period?*
KENNAN: Yes.

CHALLENER: *I noticed in one of those memoranda that you spoke of Mr. Dulles as the Republican representative in . . .*
KENNAN: Republican consultant.

CHALLENER: *Republican consultant. Yes. The adjective "Republican" was there. What I'm getting at is—did you feel at that time that he was really a participating member of the Truman-Acheson team, or someone brought in because he was a Republican?*
KENNAN: It was definitely the latter. It was an effort, I think, to get bipartisanship on the Japanese Peace Treaty, particularly because of the extreme controversial quality of relations with China.

CHALLENER: *Well, did he play the game himself? In other words, was he in agreement with what was generally being done then, or do we have a man who is getting ready for the writing of the Republican platform in 1952?*
KENNAN: Well, I think he was. And I think that actually the government went along with him all right on the Japanese Peace Treaty, which was the matter for which he particularly had been brought in, and that he rather steered clear of speaking to other questions, because he didn't want to share responsibility with the Truman administration on these other matters. That was the impression I had.

CHALLENER: *Then you sensed a little bit that he was different in his point of view?*
KENNAN: Oh, yes. He was reserved, and he wasn't saying much on the other questions. He was listening and talking outside of school, but not very much in the Department. On the other hand, I wasn't aware of any particular friction between him and Mr. Acheson at that time. They appeared to get on amiably enough.

CHALLENER: *It is a little bit of a surprise to find a man who worked with the Democrats for three or four years and then the first time you get an independent view is in that article in Life in 1952 and then the Republican platform. You just don't know how much he's been preparing the groundwork for this ahead of time.*
KENNAN: Well, I think he'd been preparing this a long time. I think this was his life's ambition, and that this was very definitely what he had in mind at the time that he came into the Department of State.

I had great respect for his mind and his ability. I recently had occasion to go through most of the 1200 pages of the testimony on the NATO Pact in the spring of 1949. I found his the only testimony that really seemed to me to be addressed to real subjects and not to legalistic ones.

On the other hand, I never shared the view that he was really a terribly pious person or that moral problems were very much on his mind, personally. I think it was useful to him politically that this image was created, but I never saw the evidences of the reality of it in action. I think he was a curious man— cold and, I think, very ambitious, and quite different in this respect from his brother, who was a warm person.

I had an unhappy experience in those first months of the Dulles administration. I can't remember exactly when it was. It was in those first months, either when I was still in Washington, or I may have gone down there for some sort of a dinner at one time. But in any case, I can remember being at a dinner where there was present one of the two younger lawyers that Mr. Dulles had brought in as his personal assistants.

CHALLENER: *Either Rod O'Connor or John Hanes.*
KENNAN: It was Mr. O'Connor.

CHALLENER: *Yes.*
KENNAN: And I found myself sitting after dinner in some sort of a little niche in somebody's drawing room with three or four people. One of them was Mr. O'Connor, and one of them was Joe Alsop. And Alsop attacked Mr. O'Connor (and with him, Mr. Dulles) so bitterly and so personally that I was much embarrassed and feared that O'Connor would have thought that I had associated myself with this or was sort of using Joe as a mouthpiece.

The next day I wrote him what I thought was a very civil little note, just saying that "I want you to know that while I have had my differences with Mr. Dulles, I did not find appropriate or well-founded the observations that Mr. Alsop made about him and would like strongly to disassociate myself from them. I am sorry that you were subjected to this sort of thing."

I never received a reply from Mr. O'Connor, which I thought was a very ungracious thing. After all, I didn't have to write him this letter.

CHALLENER: *Yes. That's right.*
KENNAN: I didn't take part in this in any way. But this was the awful atmo-

sphere that prevailed. And in those respects, it was a *most* unhappy time. What Mr. Dulles did to the Department was highly demoralizing and unhappy—an atmosphere of suspicion and coldness and cageyness was created. Everybody was on guard. Meanwhile, of course, the whole McCarthy business was roaring along in Congress; so I was just as glad to be out of it.

Well, that's about it. At some time (could it have been '51?) . . . there were the occasions of the annual Alumni Day here at Princeton. On one occasion I made the talk. On another occasion Mr. Dulles did. And I think we met on these occasions. Our talks were quite different. It seems to me he spoke the first time, and I spoke the second time.

CHALLENER: *I think that's right. I have vague recollections of that, myself.*

KENNAN: And our relations were always civil—I mean, the nearest thing we had to differences was what I've described with regard to the method of my own release.

CHALLENER: *Well, now do you have any general reactions to his policy that you'd like to comment about? Of course you've written and spoken a great deal about the nature and quality of American diplomacy in recent years, but I wondered if there was anything that . . . ?*

KENNAN: I think he handled matters very skillfully in the tactical sense. I did not object so much to what he *did* in the field of Soviet-American relations as I did to the things he *said.*

I was out of accord with the policies both of the Truman and the Eisenhower administrations with regard to NATO, and I did have occasion before I left Russia in 1952, before Mr. Dulles became Secretary of State, to write a long dispatch to the Department of State emphasizing the extent to which we had permitted the Russians to rest under the impression that NATO was an aggressive pact—the extent to which we'd really frightened them—and urging a change in the tone of NATO statements and behavior with a view to alleviating these apprehensions. This change never came, and had I remained in government I would have been, I'm sure, equally at odds with the new administration. But this was not Mr. Dulles in particular, it was just something that he never put an end to.

CHALLENER: *Well now, you just said you objected more to what he said, than what he did. Did you draw a considerable distinction between his public pronouncements and the actual policy when he was in?*

KENNAN: I do indeed! I think that Mr. Dulles with all his great qualities—this is not meant even as a critical observation—was an opportunist politically. He laid great weight on his relations with the right wing of the Republican Party in Congress. He experienced none of the discomfort and disgust, that I think I would have experienced, in playing up to those people. He was perfectly willing to do it and to do anything that really would please them. I'm sure that's the reason why he let John Davies go. And I suppose there was a superior wisdom in this. Undoubtedly this is the way to conduct policy—I mean, if you want to get domestic political backing, if that's what you put *first*. But, it didn't seem quite compatible with my ideas of leadership, you see. That's where I would have differed with him.

I must say, also, that I had *strong* differences with the Eisenhower administration, with Mr. Dulles, over the Suez crisis. I was, I think, one of the few people in our public life who came out publicly at that time in the *Washington Post*—pointing out the merit in the British position, and how bad this was of us really to mess things up in this way. But what I really held against the administration was not so much the way they behaved at that moment, but the fact that they had permitted personal relations between ourselves and the British to deteriorate to such a point where a thing like this could have happened.

This would never have happened in earlier days—I mean, at the time that I was in the State Department, in '47 to '49 and '50—as between people like myself and Oliver Franks and Roger Makins, Hume Wrong in Canada. Our relations with the British and Canadians at that time were such that misunderstandings of this magnitude could never have arisen, because anyone of us could have asked any of the others over for a drink and have said—"Let's talk this over quietly, because this is absolutely impossible."

Now, for this kind of thing, not only did the Eisenhower administration and Mr. Dulles show no appreciation, but as far as I can see they actually forebade it. They frowned on any fraternal relations of this sort with the British. This, again, I suppose was in deference to the feelings of strong elements in the Senate. It is always popular, for some reason or other, in the American legislative circles to pull the lion's tail. But I found this inexcusable to permit relations to deteriorate to the point where a thing like the Suez could happen. And, of course, it seemed to me that it had the most tragic consequences, since it occurred at exactly the same time as the Hungarian rebellion.

CHALLENER: *Did you feel that Mr. Dulles had a good understanding of the nature of Soviet Communism and the Soviet Union?*

KENNAN: Yes, I think he did. I had high respect for his understanding of international affairs generally and for his tactical skill in handling them. I don't at all doubt his enormous devotion to his work. It was his life's dream to have this position, and I think he gave it all he could. But he deferred more to Congressional opinion, with which he did not basically agree, than seemed to me to be entirely wise.

CHALLENER: *Do you think that he was so transfixed on occasion by the East-West confrontation that he couldn't see anything else except that?*

KENNAN: I think he acted that way at that time, because that was the atmosphere of the time, but he would have been just as quick to see the rise of policentrism. In fact he probably did see it.

CHALLENER: *Yes. I suspect this in his later days.*

KENNAN: You know, during those years when he was in office—I published certain things, I delivered Stafford-Little lectures here at Princeton, and I spoke over the BBC and so forth. I had the feeling that Mr. Dulles understood what I was saying probably better than—or as well as—any person in this country. And that this disconcerted him, because he knew that there was something in it, but it was all, in his opinion, much too fast for the development of Congressional opinion here and in this he was probably right. I mean, this was our respective natures. He stuck very close to the grass roots—what was possible with Congress. And I just wasn't brought up that way. I was brought up in the Executive Branch of the government. It's a different thing.

CHALLENER: *Indeed, it is.*

KENNAN: So, I don't bear him, in retrospect, any great ill will, although, I must say, he put me over some very hard bumps in that winter of 1953. It was a difficult time for me personally. It was not an easy way to leave a profession in which you had been honorably involved for a quarter of a century.

I don't think he realized—or cared enough to realize—how difficult such a thing could be for anyone else. And I think that had I ever gone down to see him—to talk to him—he would have been pleased to see me and entirely impervious to the personal effects or the damage to my career and glad to hear what I might think. But he was afraid to be associated with me. This comes out from the time when he spilled my views about the 38th parallel and the Chinese Communists in the UN. He wanted to distance himself from me all this time, because he felt that I was to some extent the daring young man on the flying trapeze. "Kennan's views," he thought, "were political idiocy. You'll never get anywhere that way."

CHALLENER: *Well, I think I've touched on everything. You've been terribly good with your time, and I appreciate this.*

Interview with George F. Kennan

Foreign Policy / 1972

From *Foreign Policy*, Summer 1972. Copyright
National Affairs. Reprinted with permission
from Foreign Policy. Copyright © 1972 by the
Carnegie Endowment for International Peace.

Q: *In the "X" article you wrote: "Now the outstanding circumstance concerning the Soviet
regime is that down to the present day this process of political consolidation has never been
completed and the men in the Kremlin have continued to be predominantly absorbed with the
struggle to secure and make absolute the power which they seized in November 1917. They
have endeavored to secure it primarily against forces at home, within Soviet society itself. But
they have also endeavored to secure it against the outside world." And you went on to state
that the "characteristics of Soviet policy, like the postulates from which they flow, are basic
to the internal nature of Soviet power, and will be with us, whether in the foreground or the
background, until the internal nature of Soviet power is changed."*

*Do you view the principal themes of Soviet policy as essentially the same today as they
were in 1947?*

A: No. The conditions to which Soviet policymakers had to address themselves in 1947 have changed drastically over these twenty-five years.

In 1947, the Soviet Union, though seriously exhausted by the war, enjoyed
great prestige. Stalin's hold on the international Communist movement was
monolithic and almost unchallenged. There was still, in the major Western
countries and to some extent elsewhere, a strong contingent of pro-Soviet
intellectuals and fellow-travellers who were amenable to Soviet influence and
could be counted on to give general support to Soviet policies. All around the
Soviet frontiers, on the other hand, there was greater instability. This applied
to East Asia as well as to Europe and the Middle East. For the Soviet leader-

ship, this presented both opportunity and danger: opportunity for taking advantage of this instability, danger that if they did not do so, others would. Their foreign policy, in these circumstances, was directed to two main objectives: one, the elimination, to the extent possible, of all other great-power influence—and this meant primarily American influence—everywhere on the Eurasian land mass, so that the Soviet Union would overshadow everything that was left, in power and prestige; and, two, the achievement and consolidation of effective strategic glacis in East, South, and West.

Compare that with the situation the present generation of Soviet leaders has before it today. The international Communist movement has broken into several pieces. They retain, beyond the limits of their own military-occupational power, the overt loyalty of only a portion of it. This is a not insignificant portion; but the facade of solidarity can be maintained, today, only by extensive concessions to the real independence of the respective Communist parties. Meanwhile, a great deal of the erstwhile liberal following in other countries, disillusioned by Soviet repressive measures at home and in Eastern Europe, has lost confidence in Soviet leadership. As a military power, the U.S.S.R. has great prestige—greater, in fact, than in 1947—but as a political power it has less than it did then.

The instability in the areas surrounding the Soviet Union has in part disappeared. The Chinese and Japanese have put an end to it in East Asia. Economic recovery, NATO, and the movements towards unification have largely done so in Western Europe, although there are disturbing symptoms of an underlying instability in Western Germany, and a state of semi-chaos in Italy that is only slightly less alarming because it is chronic.

The East Asian glacis was largely taken away from them by the Chinese. The Middle Eastern one they are gradually gaining; but it is precarious, undependable, and expensive to keep. The European one, i.e., the satellite area of Eastern and Central Europe, they continue to hold (Yugoslavia excepted) either by occupying it or by overshadowing it militarily. It is flawed by a certain potential instability in the form of the positions taken by the Rumanians; but it has won acceptance in the West, and does not appear, at the moment, to be seriously threatened. It may be said, generally, that the southern and western glacis are fulfilling their function, as does the remaining one—Outer Mongolia—in East Asia; and the Soviet leaders undoubtedly derive from this fact a certain heightened sense of security.

The effort to expel American influence and presence from the Eurasian land mass has also been largely successful, though rather by the force of circumstance than as a response to anything the Russians themselves have done. Yet the result is only in part satisfactory from the Soviet point of view. In Northeast Asia, the Americans never did play a role, except in South Korea and Japan; and they have now largely forfeited their influence over the Japanese. On the other hand, Russia now finds herself confronted there by two local great powers—China and Japan—both capable of making more trouble for her in that region than the Americans ever did. In the Middle East, the American presence and influence are pretty well eliminated everywhere except in Israel, Jordan, and Saudi Arabia. As for Western Europe: the American guaranty remains, as does the American military presence. Moscow would still like to eliminate both—just to be on the safe side. But the need for doing so has been reduced by the general acceptance of the Soviet hegemony in Eastern Europe. And the agreements concluded with the Brandt government, if ratified, will relieve the Soviet leaders of their greatest single anxiety: that of an association of American military power with a *revanchiste* and revisionist Western Germany.

If, then, today the Soviet leaders have a sense of military insecurity, it is not—for the first time in Russian history—primarily with relation to stronger forces just beyond their land borders, but rather in relation to the nuclear weapons race, which is a subject in itself. Where they really feel most insecure is politically. The Chinese inroads on their international prestige and on their influence in the world Communist movement have really hurt and alarmed them, because they leave them no alternatives except isolation or alliance with capitalist countries, which could undermine the legitimacy of their power at home. They are also insecure at home, because they are dimly conscious, as was the Tsar's regime seventy years ago, that they have lost the confidence of their own intellectuals, and don't know how to recover it. Finally, there is the continuing hostility of the populations in most of Eastern Europe to the Soviet hegemony, a hostility which even with full control of the media over twenty-five years they have not been able to overcome.

What, in the fact of these environmental conditions, are their policies? These no longer represent a unified whole, or reflect any unified concept. The Party priesthood exerts itself mightily to recover ground lost to the Chinese in the foreign Communist communities. The Foreign Office pursues a policy of detente with France and Germany and Italy in order to prove to the Chinese that Russia has an alternative to good relations with them, and can easily arrange for security on her Western front. The military-industrial complex, as real there as in Washington, struggles to match the United States in the cultivation of nuclear weaponry. The hotheads in their military establishment appear to be obsessed with the hope of breaking the long-standing supremacy of the Anglo-Americans on the high seas, and this strikes me, incidentally, as the most irresponsible and dangerous, at the moment, of all Soviet undertakings, comparable to the Kaiser's effort to out-balance the British in naval forces before World War I.

These policies present a sharp contrast to those of 1947. The Soviet-American conflict has been largely removed geographically from the Eurasian land mass and relegated to the struggle for the control of the high seas and the fantasy world of nuclear weaponry. A great part of the energy of Soviet foreign policy is today devoted to the effort to "contain," politically, another Socialist state—China. The anti-American propaganda and the competition with the United States for favor and influence in the Third World continue; but this is more of a force of habit than a policy, and the few successes achieved to date have come from American mistakes far more than from Soviet brilliance. "World revolution" has simply faded out of the picture, as a concrete aim of Soviet foreign policy. In general, the situation of the Soviet Union is such that were it not for the dangerous nuclear and naval rivalry, the outside world, and particularly, the United States, would have little more to fear from Russia today than it did in 1910. The ideological factor makes itself felt today almost exclusively in the Soviet relationship to the French and Italian Communist parties, which, if they were to come into power, would easily destroy NATO and upset the power balance in Europe. But these parties were reflections of long-term internal crises within the respective countries, and their influence cannot be treated as primarily a problem of international relations.

Q: *In what ways, if any, has "the internal nature of Soviet power" changed so as to affect Soviet policy?*
A: Stalin was well aware that the legitimacy of his ascendancy in the Party had never been wholly accepted by his comrades, that he had killed millions of people and virtually decimated the Party in his effort to crush opposition,

that he had thus provoked great potential contumacy, and that his rule rested overwhelmingly on fear. His successors are in a different position. Being largely men brought into the seats of power only towards the close of the Stalin era, they are not saddled with the same sense of guilt. Most surprisingly, furthermore—to us and to them—it turns out that the system itself is now strong enough to bear most of the weight: it does not have to depend on their charisma, as in Lenin's case, or their capacity to terrorize, as in Stalin's. Of course, they oppress the restless intellectuals. These people challenge the sense of orthodoxy that seems, to any Russian governmental mind, essential to the stability of the system. The Soviet leaders are simply acting, here, in established Russian tradition. But they are the first rulers of the Soviet Union who find themselves in the pleasing position of being able to be borne by the system—to ride along on it—instead of having to carry it; and for this reason, they feel more secure than did Lenin, who died before the system was consolidated, or Stalin, who felt it necessary to dominate it by raping it. I think, therefore, that *inner* insecurity plays less of a role in their psychology than it did in that of their predecessors, but there is strong sense of *external* insecurity, particularly with relation to the Chinese. No Leninist-Marxist can endure being outflanked to the Left, and this is what the Chinese have repeatedly done to them.

Q: *Would you today continue to emphasize "the internal nature of Soviet power," rather than the international environment, as the most pertinent factor in the making of Soviet foreign policy?*
A: No, for the reasons just given. But an exception must be made for the challenge presented by the Chinese. The position of Moscow was the "third Rome" of international Communism is little short of essential to the carefully-cultivated Soviet image of self. Take it away, and the whole contrived history of Soviet Communism, its whole rationale and sense of legitimacy, is threatened. Moscow must oppose China with real desperation, because China threatens the intactness of its own sense of identity—of the fiction on which it has made itself dependent and without which it would not know how to live.

Q: *What are the implications for American policy of these changes in Soviet internal politics and external policies?*
A: What all these means for Soviet-American relations is this: that the United

States, having accepted the Soviet domination of Eastern Europe as well as the situation in all of Asia and other than its south-eastern extremity, has today, for the first time, no serious territorial-political conflict with the Soviet government, the one exception being the Middle East. But the Middle Eastern situation is, by common agreement, not worth a war between the two powers, and both hope to avoid its leading to one. This means that today the military rivalry, in naval power as in nuclear weaponry, is simply riding along on its own momentum, like an object in space. It has no foundation in real inter-ests—no foundation, in fact, but in fear, and in an essentially irrational fear at that. It is carried not by any reason to believe that the other side *would*, but only by an hypnotic fascination with the fact that it *could*. It is simply an institutionalized force of habit. If someone could suddenly make the two sides realize that it has no purpose and if they were then to desist, the world would presumably go on, in all important respects, just as it is going on today.

There is a Kafkaesque quality to this encounter. We stand like two men who find themselves confronting each other with guns in their hands, neither with any real reason to believe that the other has murderous intentions towards him, but both hypnotized by the uncertainty and the unreasoning fear of the fact that the other is armed. The two armament efforts feed and justify each other.

Admitting that it is unreasonable to expect either side to disarm suddenly and unilaterally, one must still recognize that this curious deadlock, devoid of hope, replete with danger, is unlikely to be resolved just by carefully-negoti-ated contractual agreements: these latter will have to be supported by recipro-cal unilateral steps of restraint in the development of various forms of weaponry.

If one could begin to work this process backward, and eventually reduce the armed establishments of the two countries to something like reasonable dimensions—for both have, of course, ulterior military obligations and com-mitments as well—then there is no reason why the Soviet Union should be considered a serious threat to American security.

Should this happen, however, the United States would do well not to in-dulge itself in unreal hopes for intimacy with either the Soviet regime or the Soviet population. There are deeply-rooted traits in Soviet psychology—some of old-Russian origin, some of more recent Soviet provenance—that would rule this out. Chief among these, in my opinion, are the congenital disregard of the truth, the addiction to propagandistic exaggeration, distortion, and falsehood, the habitual foulness of mouth in official utterance. So pernicious has been the effect of fifty years of cynicism about the role of objective truth in political statement that one begins to wonder whether these Soviet leaders have not destroyed in themselves the power to distinguish truth from falsehood. The very vocabulary in which they have taught themselves to speak, politically, with its constant references to the American "imperialists" and "monopolists," is confusing and offensive, and constitutes in itself a barrier to better international understanding. Add to this the hysterical preoccupation with espionage, the continued fear of foreigners and effort to isolate the Soviet population allowed to play in the conduct of Soviet diplomacy, and one is obliged to recognize that it is simply unrealistic for Americans to look for any great intimacy or even normalcy, as we understand it, of relations with the Soviet Union. As is also the case with China, though for somewhat different reasons, relations can be reasonably good, but they must also be reasonably distant; and the more distant they are, in a sense, the better they will be.

Q: *In the "X" article you emphasized the vulnerability of the Soviet system, suggesting "that Soviet power, like the capitalist world of its conception, bears within it the seeds of its own decay." In fact, you seem to have expected "either the break-up or the gradual mellowing of Soviet power." In retrospect, was this a realistic assessment or wishful thinking on your part? And, in 1972, would you tend to emphasize the Soviet system's strengths rather than its weaknesses?*
A: I think there *has* been a very considerable mellowing of Soviet power. However little we may like the Soviet regime's internal policies, and admitting that there has recently been a considerable revival of the role of the secret police within the system, only someone who had never known the heyday of Stalin's rule could fail to recognize the enormous difference between the conditions of his time and this one.

This mellowing, I think, has been a source of strength, rather than weakness, for the Soviet regime over the short term. But any form of despotism faces, ultimately, its own dilemmas. One cannot help but notice how similar is the situation of the Soviet regime of 1972 to that of the Tsar's government in—say—1912. It has lost the confidence of the intellectuals. It is faced with a strong hard-line Stalinist opposition, chauvinistic and anti-Semitic, and comparable to the Tsarist reactionary-monarchists, which operates from *within* the official establishment; and it is faced with a liberal-democratic opposition, comparable to the old Kadet and moderate-socialist parties, which operates essentially from outside the system. Tsardom dragged along, in essentially this situation, for several decades, and then fell only when weakened by a long war and a foolish imperial couple. But the effect of modern communications has been in many respects more revolutionary than the ideas of Marx and Lenin, and whether this same longevity-by-pure-bureaucratic-inertia will be granted to the Soviet regime no one can tell. The great average age of the present Soviet leadership is also a source of potential instability. If I had to guess, I would say that the dangers confronting these present leaders are considerably greater than they themselves realize.

Q: *In your Memoirs you speak of containment as a political rather than military undertaking and express regret over the militarization of American foreign policy. Looking at the history of the past 25 years, though, wouldn't you agree that American military power has had a great deal to do with the containment of what you once called Soviet aggressive tendencies?*

A: This is an extremely difficult question. That we have taught the Soviet leadership something of our own obsession with military strength—have taught them, that is, to think in American-Pentagon terms—have caused them, too, to be hypnotized by the nuclear weapons race—I do not doubt. We also have to recognize that armaments are powerful not just in their actual use, or in support of overt threats, but also in the shadows they cast— particularly over fearful people. The Western Europeans, in particular, have a *manie d'invasion*, and I suppose it is true that if we had not eventually created some sort of compensatory ground forces, they would—in political terms— have tended ultimately "to commit suicide for fear of death." I concede, therefore, that there was need for the creation of something resembling NATO in Western Europe. But I don't think this was a reason for putting economic recovery and other constructive purposes into the background, nor was it a reason for pretending to ourselves, over two decades, that the Russians were longing to attack Western Europe, and it was only we who were deterring them from this mad purpose. Finally, I do not think the nuclear weapon was at all essential as a factor in the creation of this necessary balance. The thesis that Western Europe could never be defended against Russia by conventional means is so out of accord with all historical, economic, cultural, and demographic realities that it did not deserve to be taken seriously. The nuclear weapon is, as Stalin correctly observed, something with which you frighten people with weak nerves. We have rendered a fearful and historic disservice—to ourselves and to the world at large—by pinning our own concept of our security, and indeed the security of the entire Western world, on this ghastly, sterile, and unusable weapon, which is incapable of serving any coherent political purpose.

Q: *The expansion of Soviet influence in world affairs could take three forms: (1) direct military aggression; (2) political expansion through the seizure of power by a Communist party controlled by Moscow; or (3) diplomatic expansion through the increased influence of the U.S.S.R. in other societies by virtue of military and economic assistance, treaties, trade, cultural relations, and the like. Your notion of containment was originally concerned primarily with the possibility of the second type of Soviet expansion, although it was misinterpreted to be directed primarily against the first. In recent years, however, Soviet expansion has primarily taken the diplomatic form: increasing naval deployments in the Mediterranean and Indian Oceans, military and economic assistance to India and Arab countries, treaties with India and Egypt, expanded trade relations with many Asian and Latin American countries. Should this expansion of Soviet influence be of major concern to the United States? What policies should the United States adopt in relation to this "moving outward" by the Soviet Union?*
A: It seems to me that what you are saying in this question is that Russia is behaving suspiciously like a great power. You list a number of things she is doing: naval deployments in distant oceans, military and economic aid programs, treaties with Egypt and India, expanded trade relations with many countries. Correct. But is there any reason why a country of Russia's size and economic potential should *not* do these things? Are there, in fact, any of them that we do not do—any of them in which we have not set the example?

It seems to me that those who see a danger in these activities are predicating, just as in the case of the weapons race, some underlying political conflict which may not be there at all. I admit that Soviet activities in many of these countries are impregnated with anti-American attitudes, and one of their objectives, if not the leading one, seems to be at least the discrediting and the isolation of the United States—a purpose at which, I must say, we connive with an adeptness little short of genius. As a traditionalist who does not believe that this country is well constituted, anyway, to play a very active role in world affairs, I find myself less frightened than others over the fact that Soviet policies are so inspired.

It would be a very sad and hopeless situation if we were to convince ourselves that the peace of the world depended on the ability of the rest of us to
prevent the Soviet Union indefinitely from acting like a great power. Would
it not be better to avoid assuming that all Soviet activities are aimed primarily
against us—unless, at least, it is proved otherwise—and to see whether there
are not some areas of assistance to other nations, and constructive involvement
with their affairs, where we and the Russians could work together instead of
separately?

In saying these things one must, I suppose, make a certain exception with
respect to Soviet policies in the Middle East. In addition to the program of
naval expansion and maritime espionage, this seems to me to be the only area
of Soviet foreign relations that has been marked both by evident lack of coor-
dination in Moscow and by certain signs of a disturbing adventurism. If one
were to be asked to guess at the motives of Soviet policy from the surface
appearances, one could only conclude that Soviet policy towards the Arab
countries was based on a serious desire to gain total control over this area and
to exclude every form of Western influence. Given the existing dependence
of Western Europe on Middle Eastern oil, this represents a serious and even
dangerous challenge to the security of the Western European, and one which
seems poorly to accord with the prudence shown in other areas of the Soviet
government's foreign relations. Soviet policy-makers might do well to remind
themselves that not every fruit that seems about to fall is one which it is
desirable to pick.

Q: In Memoirs: 1925–1950 *you wrote: "What I said in the X-Article was not intended
as a doctrine. I am afraid that when I think about foreign policy, I do not think in terms of
doctrines. I think in terms of principles." There has been much talk recently about the desirability of the United States following a "balance of power" policy. Do you think this is an
appropriate and useful principle to guide U.S. policy-makers in the future? What other
principles would you recommend?*
A: If a "balance of power policy" means using American influence, wherever
possible, to assure that the ability to develop military power on the grand
scale is divided among several governmental entities and not concentrated
entirely in any one of them, then I think that I favor it. But only with two
reservations.

First of all, I think it should not be cynically conceived, and it should not, above all, be taken to mean pushing other people into conflict with each other. In this, I am fully in accord with what I understand to be the view of the present Administration.

But secondly, I would not overrate our power to affect these relationships. Twenty-five years ago we did have very considerable power to affect them, particularly in Europe, and this lay behind some of my own views about disengagement, because I thought that a better balance could be created between Russian power and a united Europe than between Russian power and a divided one. Today, except for our role in NATO, and such influence as we might have—or might have had—on the situation in the subcontinent of India-Pakistan, our possibilities are decidedly limited.

A curious balance of power does already exist today in East Asia, as between the Russians, the Chinese, and the Japanese. So long as the Russians remain strong enough to defend their own Far Eastern territories, plus Outer Mongolia, as they are today, this should assure peace along the Russian-Chinese border; and anxiety lest Japanese industrial power be added to the resources of the other party should cause both Russians and Chinese to cultivate good and peaceful relations with the Japanese. This situation is not our doing, and it needs no stimulation from us; but it serves our interests, and we should be careful not to disturb it.

Q: *In the "X" article you wrote that the ability of the United States to influence internal developments in the Communist nations, and therefore the policies they pursue, varies according to "the degree to which the United States can create among the peoples of the world generally the impression of a country which knows what it wants, which is coping successfully with the problems of its internal life and with the responsibilities of a World Power, and which has a spiritual vitality capable of holding its own among the major ideological currents of the time." Do you still believe this to be so? Given these criteria, how would you assess the record of the past twenty-five years?*

A: I do believe this to be so, but it is here that I consider we have failed most miserably. We have simply not faced up successfully to our own internal problems; and we have lost, just since World War II, a great deal of our value, and our potential influence, as an example to other peoples. So obvious is this that if, thinking about the worldwide loss of American prestige and influence in recent years, one asks whether the Russians have succeeded in setting us back, one has to give the answer: no—we and the Russians have each defeated ourselves; neither was up to its own pretensions of earlier years.

Q: *How well do the Nixon-Kissinger policies for dealing with the Communist nations seem to fit the notions which underlay your own thinking at the time of the "X" article and subsequently?*

A: The Nixon-Kissinger policies fit the conceptions of the "X" article, it seems to me, only indifferently.

Those policies continue to give great attention, geographically, to what I viewed in 1947, and have always viewed, as a secondary area from the standpoint of our interests: Southeast Asia.

While the SALT talks are certainly a significant and welcome step in advance, a great deal of American governmental attention and energy continues to be riveted to the sterile and dangerous effort to excel the Russians in the nuclear arms race. That had no place in my scheme of things.

There is undue emphasis on China, from which we have very little to gain in terms of world policy, and a certain slighting, in my view, of Japan.

You may say that much of this is not responsive to your question, which involved our dealings with the Communist nations, directly. But it has always been true that the secret of successful dealings with Russia itself—and the same now goes for China—is the proper handling of our relations with the remainder of the world that lies between us.

Finally, there is the obvious partiality for summit meetings with Communist leaders, a procedure which may have its domestic-political dividends but which I regard as at best irrelevant, and potentially pernicious, to a sound handling of relations with the great Communist governments.

So far as the Soviet Union itself is concerned, I do not see a great deal that the Nixon Administration could do that it is not now doing. I think—though it may not be of major importance—that we should at once agree to the cessation of underground testing. I think that we could well take certain further unilateral measures of restraint in the development of nuclear weapons and their carriers, with a view to encouraging the others to do likewise. I think we should press talks with the Russians to see whether we could not agree with them on putting a stop to the childish and dangerous mutual shadowing of naval vessels that now goes on all over the high seas. I think we should bend every effort to develop technical collaboration with them—in space activities as well as in international environmental undertakings. We should keep in communication with them—constantly—concerning the situation in the

Middle East, with a view to avoiding misunderstandings. Beyond that, there is not much we can do.

Q: *In the light of its subsequent misinterpretation, do you regret having written the "X" article?*

A: No—not on balance. I regret having written it exactly the way I did. But it was meant to sound—and did sound, I think, at the time—a hopeful note, urging people to believe that our differences with the Soviet Union of Stalin's day, while serious indeed, were not ones that could be solved only—or indeed, solved at all—by war. Well—we have struggled along for another quarter of a century, and there has been no war—at least not between us and the Russians. And there is even less reason to think one necessary today than there was then.

The importance of the "X" article was of course distorted out of all reasonable proportion by the treatment it received at the hands of the press. The American mass media produced upon any given event an effect analogous to that produced on a man's shadow by the angle of the sun—causing it normally be either much greater or much less than life-size. In the case of this particular article it was much greater.

But the principle enunciated in it—that our differences with the Russians are not ones which it would take a war to solve—is still sound. What we need mostly to do is to free ourselves from some of our fixations with relation to the military competition—to remind ourselves that there is really no reason why we and the Russians should wish to do frightful things to each other and to the world—and to address ourselves vigorously, and with some degree of boldness, to the enormous danger presented by the very existence in human hands, and above all the proliferation, of weapons such as the nuclear ones. Somewhere between the intimacy we cannot have—either with the Russians or the Chinese—and the war there is no reason for us to fight, there is a middle ground of peaceful, if somewhat distant, coexistence on which our relationship with the great Communist powers could be considerably safer and more pleasant than it now is. We cannot make it so by our own efforts alone; the Russians and Chinese will have to help. But we could do better, in a number of respects, than we have been doing.

Conversation with George Kennan

Eric Sevareid / 1975

From *Conversations with Eric Sevareid* (Washington, D.C.: Public Affairs Press, 1976). Copyright © 1976 by CBS NEWS, a division of CBS Broadcasting, Inc. All rights reserved. Reprinted by permission.

SEVAREID: *Some serious students of foreign affairs have called George Kennan America's most professional diplomat and our foremost scholar of Russia. Others have called him the "Architect of the Cold War." For more than thirty years he has ranked high among the best of American diplomats. He specialized in Soviet affairs. In 1952 he received the appointment to which all his training had led—Ambassadorship to Moscow. But his expertise was troublesome to Stalin: Kennan knew too much. Within six months the Soviet leader found a pretext to kick him out.*

Back in Washington a new Republican administration looked without favor on Kennan's service under the Democrats. Secretary of State John Foster Dulles, a colder warrior by many years, refused to reassign Kennan, who then resigned from the Foreign Service. Since then Kennan has devoted himself to scholarship. Though respected by diplomats and scholars, he remains a controversial figure among politicians. A short time ago he and I spent some hours talking at the Institute for Advanced Study in Princeton.

George Kennan is a diplomat whose public career was abruptly ended by warriors much more bellicose than he. But for anyone who has read the books he has written he can be called a prophet with less honor than he should have received. For many years he saw American foreign policy ahead of its formulation and execution. He still does.

A high point of American relations with the Soviet Union was reached in 1945, when the First United States Army and the First Ukranian Army met at the River Elbe. It seemed as if the two greatest nations on earth were locked forever in mutual friendship. Yet two years later friendship had turned to irritation and shapeless, undefined hostility began to appear.

144

The favorite magazine for diplomats is Foreign Affairs. *In July 1947 an unsigned article appeared in its pages. Its title was "The Sources of Soviet Conduct." Its author was "X"—really George Kennan. And this is what he had to say: "Any United States policy toward the Soviet Union must be that of firm and vigilant containment of Russian expansive tendencies. It is clear that the United States cannot expect in the foreseeable future to enjoy political intimacy with the Soviet Regime." American policy, Kennan continued, should be designed "to confront the Russians with unalterable counter-force at every point . . ." Thus the ideology of the Cold War was anticipated by this scholar-diplomat.*

But we must begin back in the days just after he invented the term "containment." The containment that came was not the containment he wanted. We asked him, "What were you getting at when you wrote that famous article in Foreign Affairs?"

KENNAN: What I thought was essential in 1945, in 1946, and in 1947 was to prevent the political influence and predominant authority of the Soviet Government from spreading any further in the world, because we had had it demonstrated in the period of World War II that you didn't always have to occupy another country in order to dominate its life. You could threaten it, or you could subvert its government by various ways, including the time-honored phenomenon of puppet government. I was afraid, I must say, at that time (and I think with some reason) of what is today called the "domino theory." Western Europe, as the war ended, was in a sorry state. People were disoriented, discouraged, apprehensive, frightened by the experiences of the war, and it would not have been too difficult for Italy or for France, if they had lost their confidence in us then, to turn to the Soviet Union and let their Communist parties take over. It seemed to me that it was important for Europe, for us, and, in the long run, even for the Russians—that this should not happen. It just wasn't desirable.

When I talked about containment, what I had in mind was an effort on our part to stiffen the hope, the confidence, of European Nations in themselves, and to persuade them that they didn't need to yield to one great power or another, that they could resume life. We would help them to do it. That was all that was involved. I didn't think the Russians wanted to attack anyone. I didn't think they wanted to expand any further by force of arms. I'm sure I was absolutely right about this. In 1948, when the talk of the formation of the NATO pact began (it was actually the Europeans—the French and the British and the Benelux people—who came to us and wanted it) I was quite surprised. I said, "Why are you giving your attention to this? We're just getting the

Marshall Plan through. For goodness sake, concentrate on your economic recovery. Nobody's going to attack you." But I found that all of Western Europe had what the French call "la manie d'invasion"—the mania of invasion.

SEVAREID: *That's what revisionists forget. It was the Europeans who were terrified to death at this period.*
KENNAN: That's correct.

SEVAREID: *They're less terrified than we are today, but at that time it was quite the reverse. But are you saying, in effect, that you didn't think NATO (the North Atlantic Treaty Organization) was really necessary then? The other theory was that unless you had a military shield this economic development wouldn't go forward in peace.*
KENNAN: Within the course of time the military shield probably would have had to be built, although it never had to assume the dimensions that it has today. I think one could have dealt with the Russians about these things. At any rate, it should never have been given the emphasis it was given. We should never have allowed the thesis to become established that, if it were not for the so-called deterrent quality of our nuclear weapons, the Russians would immediately have attacked Western Europe and overrun it. I never thought this was true.

SEVAREID: *But wasn't it true that at this period you really did not want to see Germany armed? You wanted, I thought, a neutralized and possibly unified Germany. That was the seat of the whole argument, wasn't it?*
KENNAN: That's correct. The reason that this was so ill received in the Western countries (above all in Western Germany itself, in England, even in the neutral countries of Switzerland and Sweden) was that people in Europe were still more afraid of the Germans than they were . . . Put it this way: they put a higher value on American defense against the Germans than they did on the retirement of the Soviet forces from Eastern Europe. And they really didn't want the removal of the split of the continent. You must realize that this dividend continent suited—and still suits—many people in Western Europe very well because, as they see it, the present arrangement means that we defend them both against the Russians and the Germans. It leaves the whole onus on this country.

SEVAREID: *You're really talking about the French here?*
KENNAN: Yes, and the English, the Dutch. They don't want to make the sacri-

fices that are necessary to defend themselves in Western Europe. They have the population. They have the industrial strength to keep forces fully adequate to the defense of Western Europe. They're not deficient in either of these.

SEVAREID: *But as long as we're there with an atomic shield and trip wire, they're not going to do it.*
KENNAN: That's right. It gives them an excuse for not maintaining conventional forces at the requisite level.

SEVAREID: *But our official line now in the Pentagon (and I suppose the State Department) is that were we not there with these troops, they wouldn't pull together and contribute more; they would just go apart.*
KENNAN: Well, a great deal of water has flown over the dam since the days when we argued about these things. But I will tell you two reasons why I was reluctant to see us perpetuate the division of Germany and of Europe. One was the Berlin situation, which didn't fit in with a divided Europe. I regarded Berlin as the greatest single danger spot in Europe and I thought we were going to have trouble with this if we tried to divide the continent on the present line. But the other reason is today an even more serious reason—our willingness to see the division of the continent perpetuated really consigned all the Eastern European countries by implication to the Russian sphere. Now that was, of course, rough on them, but it's also questionable how long it will last, how long it will stick. If any of these countries ever does succeed in liberating itself from the Soviet sphere of influence then our scheme of things is going to have no place for it.

SEVAREID: *They have no place to go.*
KENNAN: We have a Western European alliance. If we try to take an Eastern European country into it that's going to be a real military provocation for the Russians. They could not stand it.

SEVAREID: *I thought you really never believed that they could or would liberate themselves.*
KENNAN: I never believed that it was our duty to liberate them but I cannot guarantee to the Russians that they will be able to bear this burden successfully forever. This is a very unnatural thing. They're sitting on ninety million people with a higher standard of living and a more Western cultural tradition than their own and there is restlessness. There's no doubt about it. A lot of people

in these countries don't like it. There is practically no real communist enthusiasm in Eastern Europe from the Baltic Sea to the Black Sea.

SEVAREID: *What about the other side of the line? What happens if Portugal comes under Communist domination? Italy?*
KENNAN: That's a good question. I am sure that what is happening in Portugal presents very considerable problems for people in Moscow. In some ways I can see that they might like the Communist Party there to take charge of things but in other respects the situation in the world is such today that I'm not sure they really want this to happen. Instability in Western Europe could mean instability in Eastern Europe today and instability in Portugal could mean instability all along the northern littoral of the Mediterranean. After all, Spain next door is very closely connected with Portugal, Spain is now entering a period of great uncertainty. Obviously, the period that has existed there since the termination of the civil war is coming to an end and nobody knows what is going to happen in Spain in the coming period. What happens in Portugal certainly is going to influence it. Then you have Italy almost effectively without a government today. And you have the Greeks and the Turks at each other's throats and the Cyprus situation.

SEVAREID: *Everybody in Washington sees it as a great setback for us, destabilizing our whole arrangement for Europe. But you're saying this is also very destabilizing for the Russians?*
KENNAN: Yes, the Soviet leadership is an old leadership. The average age of the top five people is well over seventy. They have many problems at home, they have problems with their zone of influence in Eastern Europe, and I think they want things kept quiet.

SEVAREID: *Partly because of China, I suppose?*
KENNAN: Because of China, too. Very important. I'm glad you mentioned that. I think that a stable Western Europe has certain virtues in the Soviet eyes in view of their relations with China. I don't mean to oversimplify this. I think it pulls both ways. One of the great dangers that we are up against now is that if the situation deteriorates further in Portugal and along the northern shores of the Mediterranean there will be voices—there probably are already voices—being raised in the Communist part of the world which say, "What are we waiting for? What's the matter with us? Why don't we let this balloon

go up? We have the best situation for revolutionary activity in Western Europe that we've had since 1945 or 1946. Are we not missing a great chance if we don't inspire the Italian Communist Party now to use its great popular strength and to seize power? Perhaps the French as well?" This is a very delicate situation.

SEVAREID: *But you don't mean that this necessarily makes an addition to Soviet power in the world?*
KENNAN: What is happening in Portugal does make a difference for Soviet power because it raises a very serious question for NATO. And I am rather surprised that the NATO countries have not already taken more account of this than they have. I think what's happening in Portugal is absolutely tragic. I don't think this is by nature a country destined or suited for a Communist dictatorship. But it may fall to its Communist party.

SEVAREID: *You said back in 1968 that you didn't understand talk about detente. Now, that's all we hear about.*
KENNAN: This whole question of detente is being rapidly undermined and made out of date by the developments that are now occurring in the world—by the energy crisis, by what's happening in Portugal, by what's happening in Indochina. We're entering a new era. I don't think the Russians are going to have the same interest in having detente with us as distinct with having it with the Western Europeans. I think we'll see them shift the burden of their talk about detente from the United States to Western Europe. In other words, they will say, "Well, what we want is detente with the West generally" but actually they will apply it to West Germany and France.

SEVAREID: *You see signs of that now?*
KENNAN: Yes, one sees already signs of it.

SEVAREID: *We now have a whole spate of so-called revisionist historians in this country. The premise of many of them is that the United States was really responsible for the Cold War. We started it and we perpetrated it. The Russians would have behaved very, very differently and things would be different today if it weren't for the Cold War. What do you think about this? What do you think the Russian aims were at the end of the war?*
KENNAN: I think they hoped, and very much wanted, to get us out of the Eurasian continent entirely so that they would have no Great Power opponent to themselves. This I felt we had to resist. It was a hope which they expected

to implement, as I said before, through the Communist parties, not through further military attacks.

SEVAREID: *Of course, Western Europe was pretty flat, and we did take our troops back; it was a long time before we returned them to Europe. The Russians were reaching into the German Ruhr, in North Africa, and many other places.*

KENNAN: Yes, they were, and much of their behavior indicated to me a desire, first of all, to get us out; secondly, to get control of the German industrial district of the Ruhr; thirdly, to prevent the revival of a vigorous economic life and political confidence in Western Europe. It seemed to me that we had to combat all these things. We had at that time—and these young people who write the revisionist books forget about this—some terrible examples of what Communist rule could mean to a foreign people over which it was extended. Some of us had never forgotten what was done to the Poles in the fall of 1939 and 1940. Some 800 or 900 thousand people were evidently deported from eastern Poland after the Soviet troops came in under the most abominably cruel circumstances. I don't think half of these Poles were ever heard from again. These were not people who had taken any military action against Russia. They were eliminated solely on the basis of what was believed to be their social coloration. So I must say that some of us had a lively horror of what was going to happen in other areas of Europe if the Russians took them under their control.

SEVAREID: *Is there a vast difference between Stalin and his people and the present crowd in Moscow?*

KENNAN: I think there is a very great difference. What happened in Stalin's time was absolutely nightmarish. It was totalitarianism at its most hideous and horrible. After all, somewhere in the neighborhood of nine to eleven million people were probably executed or caused to die in one way or another, unnaturally, by this regime in the course of a few years. That is a terrible indictment of any regime.

SEVAREID: *You mean before World War II?*

KENNAN: Before, during, and after. Even during World War II the repression of the population was terrible.

SEVAREID: *That was one reason, wasn't it, for the apparent great bravery of Russian soldiers in the war? They didn't retreat.*

KENNAN: Yes. People have never understood the causes of the behavior of the Red Army. I don't say that they didn't fight for patriotism in many instances. Indeed, they did. But they were also under the most terrible sort of discipline. They were often put in impossible military situations where to remain and fight it out was almost surely to get killed. Yet to retreat was to be shot by their own people. To get taken prisoner was to be punished when they were finally repatriated. Their choices were almost impossible.

SEVAREID: *I think Stalin said to Harriman once that it took more courage for a Russian soldier to retreat than to advance.*
KENNAN: There's something to that.

SEVAREID: *We've had, I guess, two great movements in modern life—Christianity and Communism. I can't see that Christianity spread a lot of peace and love over the human race or that Communism has spread a lot of fraternity and equality. What is the grip of this notion? Even in prosperous Western free lands there are quite a number of youngsters who are utterly gripped by Marxist socialism in spite of all that Solzhenitsyn has written, in spite of the total obliteration of the human individual in China. How do you explain this?*
KENNAN: I can only explain it as a sublimated form of an aversion to modern Western society, to its materialism, to its lack of ideals, to its continued appeal to the acquisitive and selfish aims of people rather than to their capacity for self-sacrifice and devotion to public aims. I think all of us have let the youth down to some extent. This, really, rather than any understanding of Marxian doctrine, is what causes them to mouth Communist slogans.

SEVAREID: *How much hope should we put on the present dissident movements in the Soviet Union?*
KENNAN: I don't think much short-term hope, but I would put very serious long-term hope in them because they are filling a vacuum which the Soviet Government has never contrived to fill. A moment ago you mentioned Communism as one of the very movements which has moved mankind and Christianity as the other. Well, it's quite true that Christianity had its aggressive phases, the Church did, and created trouble as well as other things. But I remember Chip Bohlen saying to me, back in the 1930s, that in the end Communism is bound to fail as an ideological appeal to people because it has no answer to the phenomenon of death, and Christianity does. I think this is true. I think there is something in Marxism that causes a certain lack of appeal in

the long run, that has to be filled with something else, and that is beginning to be filled with the strong, stern, moral sense of obligation that fills many of the dissidents and, outstandingly, Solzhenitsyn.

SEVAREID: *Well, the Bible said this long ago: You can't live by bread alone.*
KENNAN: Exactly. And the Marxist doctrine is a materialist doctrine. Now you may say, yes, but we just referred to the great popularity of this doctrine throughout large parts of the world. But such popularity doesn't exist among the people who have been subjected to it as a political regime. You'll find more Communists among American liberal youth or Norwegian liberal youth than you will, proportionately, among Communists in Eastern Europe and Russia.

SEVAREID: *You've had two famous careers—one as a diplomat and one as a scholar and writer of diplomacy and history. You're buried away now in the Smithsonian Institution writing about pre-World War I. I wonder why this period.*
KENNAN: Some years ago I wrote two volumes on the early period of Soviet-American relations. These first months of Soviet-American relations were also the last year of World War I. It was borne in on me, through writing those books, that World War I really caused a great many of the troubles of the remainder of the century. For one thing, it produced the Russian Revolution. The more I thought about this, the more I came to view World War I as the fundamental catastrophe of this century.

In England, in France and in Germany, during the twenty years that followed World War I, you saw the absence of the mature father's generation. Politics divided oldsters like Hindenburg and Petain and the young Nazis in the street. What was lacking was the mature generation of men who should have been in the prime of their life and in the fullness of their strength. They simply were not there.

SEVAREID: *You're saying that there was a kind of a break in continuity between generations which made Hitler more possible?*
KENNAN: Yes, indeed. Had those men—the two million men who were killed on the German side in World War I—had they been around as mature men during the thirties, I'm convinced the Nazis would never have been able to take over as they did.

SEVAREID: *They wouldn't have been so anxious to goosestep again.*
KENNAN: That's right. Europe did profound violence and damage to the fabric

of its own life, even genetically and in the balance of generations, by the bloodshed of World War I. No issue which was at stake in that war could possibly have justified the hounding of eight million young men into rat-ridden, muddy trenches to be slaughtered off there by artillery fire. This was madness. There was nothing at stake in the war which could have justified their deaths in this way.

SEVAREID: *Mr. Kennan, you've had an immense amount of psychic remuneration in your life, a great deal of admiration and praise and awards of every kind, both for your diplomacy and your writing. There's also been a running criticism of your general stance about diplomacy in this century. You've been described as someone who really thinks diplomacy should be left to a kind of priestly cult, people think you're much too much of a perfectionist and a moralist. How do you see yourself in relation to those complaints?*

KENNAN: Well, there are a lot of different things embraced in what you've just said. As far as diplomacy being a priestly cult is concerned, I, in my turn, wonder about the evident conviction of political Washington that, although almost every other responsible profession requires professional training and experience, diplomacy should not. I don't know why it's necessary to have professional training and experience to be an attorney or a doctor or a number of other things, but it should not be required for diplomacy. I think there is great room for the professionals in diplomacy. I think they should have the overwhelming bulk of the jobs in this field. I do not feel that they should have exclusive control over it. I can see room for the talented nonprofessional. I can see why Presidents might want to be represented abroad at times by people who are close friends of theirs, provided that these people have the necessary educational and cultural level to represent the country credibly. But I hold a strong brief for professionalism in foreign affairs. And I think one of the troubles today with the State Department and the Foreign Service is that they have been administered for decades by people who had no knowledge or experience of the substance of their work.

SEVAREID: *But I think you once said that you feel most at home in the eighteenth century, an era of order and reason, a period of a hard-headedness in foreign policy.*

KENNAN: Well, that is true, but I am anything but an egalitarian. I am very much opposed to egalitarian tendencies of all sorts in governmental life and in other walks of life. Sometimes I've been charged with being an elitist. Well, of course, I am. What do people expect? God forbid that we should be without an elite. Is everything to be done by gray mediocrity? After all, our whole system is based on the selection of people for different functions in our life. When you talk about selection, you're talking about an elite.

SEVAREID: *There's another approach that lots of people want to take—you still hear about it—and that's the so-called "people to people" idea. President Eisenhower tried to organize this sort of thing with the notion that if all kinds of ordinary people crossed lots of borders and mixed with foreigners somehow we'd come to know each other better, somehow you'd have more peace and get along better.*

KENNAN: This is a very attractive and almost moving but naive idea. I don't think that this necessarily contributes to better understanding. I think that, ideally, it would be better if these contacts could be maintained by people who had some preparation for it.

SEVAREID: *What do you think of one-man diplomacy? It really began with Dulles. He was travelling everywhere. And then Rusk came in and said privately he was not going to do that, he was going to run things from Washington—and he travelled even more than Dulles. Now Kissinger's broken all records.*

KENNAN: Well, that's a very hard question. There are both pros and cons in the case of Henry Kissinger. He had two situations so unusual and so terrible that it really did require, I think, the personal self-insertion of a very high figure in our government to get anywhere. One of them was the liquidation, as we thought, of our involvement in Southeast Asia, and the other was the dangerous situation in the Middle East. I cannot bring myself to blame Kissinger seriously for involving himself in these two situations. I think he did it with extraordinary skill, fortitude, tact, and dedication; he deserves a lot of credit for this. But on principle, and except for very rare situations of this sort, I think the best thing the Secretary of State can do is sit right there in his chair and survey and direct the whole great spectrum of our foreign relations day by day, and let somebody else do the travelling. I don't think he should even go to all the NATO meetings and things like this that he's asked to go to.

SEVAREID: *What about the summit meetings? Apparently one is coming up before too long.*

KENNAN: I'm sorry if it goes against the grain of people in Washington but I do not approve of summit meetings, except for purposes of courtesy and to ratify agreements arrived at, and, even then, I think they have certain adverse effects which I don't like. The President is a man who sits in the thick of a welter of duties and responsibilities. He has to be at one and the same time a protocol head of state, a prime minister, and a party leader. I don't think these three offices should be combined in one man, but if they're going to be then the man should not absent himself for days on end, occupying himself with only one single question.

SEVAREID: *I'm thinking of something Adlai Stevenson said when he was at the UN as Ambassador. He said that international diplomacy was one-third alcohol, one-third protocol and one-third Geritol. He was exhausted with it.*

You've been criticized occasionally as one who just cannot accept the effect of domestic politics on foreign policy. I don't know any way that you can completely separate these things.
KENNAN: I don't so much criticize the effect in itself. But if a government (in this case our government) cannot refrain from conducting foreign policy for domestic political reasons, instead of with a view to the general interests of the country at large, then it should restrain itself in the ambitiousness of the policies it tries to implement.

SEVAREID: *Here we are a big power but acting on impulses that are essentially parochial in many cases.*
KENNAN: Exactly. The impulses represent the interests only of one portion of our population which can speak loudest or bring the heaviest pressures to bear on Congress.

SEVAREID: *Are you thinking of things like Senator Jackson's amendment on the immigration of Jews from Russia as one of those things?*
KENNAN: I certainly do. I don't think there was any general American interest involved here at all and yet, we were asked to sacrifice, and did sacrifice, a good deal to these impulses of Senator Jackson's. We sacrificed the trade bill to them.

SEVAREID: *One of the handicaps we have, of course—at least vis-à-vis the Russians—is that we can't do things secretly.*
KENNAN: Well, this too, is a very important subject. I'm very unhappy about the way the CIA has been treated in the press. Obviously, mistakes were made, serious mistakes, but they were the affair of a tiny proportion of the whole great apparatus of CIA. It seems to me absolutely tragic. I have known

many people in the agency. I had to work with them when I was in government. The CIA has a host of talented, well-informed and highly devoted government servants who have never done anything but the most legitimate sort of work. For all of them to be tagged with the tag of sinisterism is senseless. It seems to me to be a little short of tragic.

SEVAREID: *How would you define the role of the CIA as you think it really ought to be?*
KENNAN: I think it should be primarily the scholarly study of the rest of the world and of what's happening in the world generally on the basis of legitimate sources. We discovered many years ago, those of us in the Russian field, that when we made a careful study of conditions in Russia in the way any other scholar would—on the basis of material that was available to us in legitimate ways, either in the press or through legitimate sources of observation—as a rule we knew much more than did the gumshoe agents who tried to find out things by secret operations. I think that remains true today.

But the fact of the matter is that all this can't stop just at our borders. We have, I believe, about a million, if not more, people in this country who are not even American citizens. A great many of them are here illegally. They entered clandestinely. Foreign governments operate among these people. We have every right to keep an eye on what foreign governments are doing in this country.

SEVAREID: *As to CIA operations abroad, do you really think we ought to be in the business of trying to knock over other governments?*
KENNAN: No. I must say that I favor the termination of secret political operations, as distinct from secret intelligence gathering abroad. I say this not because I think that there's never a place for it. I think there have been cases where we had a legitimate reason to want to do this, where it should have been done quietly and secretly. But I am against it because if you can't keep things like this secret you shouldn't do them at all. And if our system, as is evidently the case, is incapable of keeping these things secret over the long run then it better not get into this game at all.

SEVAREID: *Well, now we come back to the thing that has haunted this country for the last dozen years and torn us up badly—morally, economically, politically—and that's Vietnam. Since about the fall of 1965 I've been sure that Vietnam was a mistake. I think you were on record in the State Department pretty early as saying, "Don't get involved in it." Is that correct?*

KENNAN: That is correct. Of course, I was on record mostly through a whole day spent on television before the Senate Foreign Relations Committee.

SEVAREID: *What was your argument then?*
KENNAN: Well, I liked to quote the marvelous statement of John Quincy Adams given in an obscure Fourth of July speech. I fished it out, and it has since been used by many people: "America is the friend of the liberties of all the world. She is the guardian only of her own."

SEVAREID: *What was the real reasoning—if there was coherent reasoning behind it—that this would be an extension of Chinese power and that they were expansionist and aggressive and a danger to us?*
KENNAN: I can only go back to the hypnotic power of the Cold War syndrome as it was—as it imposed itself on American political life at the time of the McCarthyism, at the time of the row over our policy toward China. Since that time, it seems to me, every American administration has been afraid of being accused of not having stood up to something which is described as "Communism." Well, in 1945, we knew what that was.

Today when someone says "Communism," I have to say, "What Communism?" because a host of things go under this name—Tito, the Chinese Communists, Castro, and all sorts of cliques and groups of people in other parts of the world. But people here are still hypnotized by this word, apparently hypnotized by the rather silly statement that America never lost a war and that it would be somehow intolerable. That's not really true. Who won and who lost in the War of 1812 or the Korean War? It's useless to put questions in such terms. Yet this can be done; it's a sort of a challenge in Washington. If you fling it at someone he reacts automatically.

SEVAREID: *Suppose all of Indochina really is going to be in Communist hands. What's the danger to us there?*
KENNAN: Well, I can't see that there is any. This is a feeling I've had ever since the late forties and have stated since the late forties. For the time being, we won't have the same opportunities of sending businessmen and missionaries and all sorts of busybodies to this area. I don't think we're going to suffer very greatly from that. They're going to need trade, just as all other Communist countries do. We'll trade with them, eventually, to the extent that we want to. I think that we're greatly exaggerating the ills that would befall us.

SEVAREID: *It never seemed to me that, whatever the ills might turn out to be, they had any relationship to the price we were paying for intervention.*
KENNAN: The price was appalling. It's rather like the retirement of the European colonial powers from their colonial possessions. They thought there was going to be a terrible loss of prestige but there wasn't.

It's my view that if today we were to take all our cards back into our hand and reduce our commitments to something resembling our ability to make good on those commitments, that our prestige in the world would only be heightened, rather than weakened. I think we couldn't lose anything at all by cutting a whole series of unsound commitments.

SEVAREID: *I heard Mr. Kissinger not long ago say in his anguish about Vietnam that peace is indivisible. This is a phrase the Russians began to use, as I remember, back in the Popular Front days or about the time they were getting scared of Hitler.*
KENNAN: It was Litvinov who used to say this.

SEVAREID: *I suppose it was true, more or less—*
KENNAN: No, I don't think it was true at all.

SEVAREID: *In Hitler's time?*
KENNAN: I don't think it's ever been true. It's a very terrible doctrine because it means that no conflicts can be isolated. Since human nature has been cantankerous and unreasonable from the beginning, there are always going to be conflicts between groups of people in this world. The only safety for humanity lies in the possibility of isolating the conflicts and preventing them from getting to be bigger ones. Therefore, anyone who says that peace is indivisible puts upon the international community the onus of solving every last minor scrap.

SEVAREID: *That's like saying freedom is indivisible. It always seemed to me that the two— peace and freedom—are very divisible. They will co-exist with war and tyranny, which they have during most of history.*
KENNAN: Of course.

SEVAREID: *Another thing about our policy since World War II, it seems to have been based on the premise that peace, material prosperity, and democracy were all not just good, each in itself, but interdependent, interlinked. But you have a totalitarian dictatorship like East Germany that's very prosperous. I don't see the connection, but that seems to be the theme.*

KENNAN: There is none. There is no connection at all. I am constantly amazed at the persistence of the view in this country that democracy is the natural state of mankind, and that there is something wrong, that we have been in some way remiss, if other countries don't have it.

I don't think this is true. I think that democracy is a form of government which has found its seat, you might say in a broad sense, among the countries or people who had their origins on the shores of the North Sea, and that it has never been very common elsewhere.

SEVAREID: *I know the Mideast has not been your specialty in your career but Russia has been. The two impinge very much. A lot of people now think we've been over our heads in the Mideast, that we cannot settle things without the Russians at some ultimate stage of the matter. Is there any chance of bringing the Russians in or do they just want the exacerbation of tensions?*

KENNAN: I think there would be a very good chance of talking with the Russians, and, at least, of preventing the Mideastern situation from developing into a world war. I think the Russians are very anxious to see something like that happen. But I must say that I find myself somewhat inhibited in speaking about our policy toward the Middle East. This is obviously a field of American policy in which we are not completely masters of ourselves. I think we have to first recover the full independence of our own policy. We have to make a certain declaration of independence from at least the lobbyists, the Zionist lobbyists, in this country before we can treat this question as it should be treated. Once we have declared that independence and once we act on behalf of the country as a whole and its interests, then I would like to see us show the greatest deference to the need for preserving the existence of the state of Israel and for preventing a second massacre of Jews in our own time.

SEVAREID: *Very recently, Daniel Patrick Moynihan wrote a rather electric article in* Com-mentary *about the so-called Third World countries, all the small countries but including the raw-material countries, saying, "Stop taking their abuse. Stop feeling guilty toward them. We really don't owe them very much, if anything. Stand up for America in these debates in the UN, UNESCO and the population and food conferences and so on." I think you said this a good twenty years ago.*

KENNAN: For some reason or other we have tried for twenty years to ingratiate ourselves with these people and to please them as though we were the suppli-cant party, as though we depended on them and not they on us. I think we really have to stop this now and let them come to their own assessment of how much we mean to them.

SEVAREID: *Sometimes I despair of ever pleasing any of them. We've been trying to please them for years and years, in Latin America or wherever. They accuse us of extracting their wealth, their raw materials, getting rich off them, impoverishing them in effect. And then, when we go back—as we're now doing through the multi-national corporations—and put our factories right in those countries and use their materials there and create employment and help educate and start small business and all the rest, then we're equally denounced for putting some kind of octopus over them and running their lives.*

KENNAN: Yes, there's a certain hysteria abroad among them today, a certain anti-American hysteria. In my opinion this won't be cured until we call their bluff and leave them alone.

SEVAREID: *You mean even foreign economic aid? Stop it?*

KENNAN: I certainly do. Most of it, I think, could be terminated, especially the arms aid. You know, what I would really like to see—it sounds extreme—but I would like to see a statement on the part of this government that, within a reasonable period (let's say five years), it would become our policy not to export any arms to anyone under any circumstances.

SEVAREID: *Whether the Soviets do it or not?*

KENNAN: Yes.

SEVAREID: *That doesn't add to their power particularly.*

KENNAN: These people are going to get the arms anyway, whether we send them or not.

SEVAREID: *You've been saying many things that add up to the notion that we mustn't let our reach exceed our grasp and we mustn't be defensive toward everybody in the world. Is that what you mean by neo-isolationism?*

KENNAN: Yes, it is. I'm under no illusions that we could completely wall ourselves off from the rest of the world but I would like to see us make ourselves a great deal more independent when it comes to energy and other commodities vital to the success of our national life. I think we ought to have a period of withdrawal from a great many of our involvements if only to prove to other people that we're not trying to do something terrible to them. I don't think

they'll believe it, I don't think they'll get over this complex of American impe-
rialism, until we say to them: "Very well, we're willing to leave you entirely
alone. We'll go home. You take your time. If you ever feel the time has come
when you need the United States again, come and tell us. We'll think about
it."

A Major Voice in the Debate over Nuclear Arms

U.S. News & World Report / 1982

On April 7, four former high United States officials stunned Washington by calling for a pledge that America would never be the first to resort to nuclear arms. To find out more about the proposal, *U.S. News & World Report* to one of the four—a man who thirty-five years ago, at the outset of the cold war, was the architect of the U.S. policy of containing Soviet expansionism.

Q: *Mr. Kennan, you have proposed that the United States renounce the use of atomic weapons as an option in any future war. Why are you making that proposal?*
A: For one simple reason: The number of nuclear arms in the superpowers' arsenals is so great and so horrendous that the risk has become unacceptable. To initiate atomic war, even on a small scale, would be a profound gamble. The damage that would result from escalation to an all-out nuclear exchange is difficult to assess but probably beyond belief. It would shatter Western civilization.

One mustn't play with such a possibility. By clinging to a "first use" option, we are, in fact, doing precisely that. It's time to finally put this idea behind us.

Q: *Wouldn't that mean the end of Washington's thirty-year strategy for using battlefield nuclear weapons, if necessary, to stop a massive Soviet conventional attack on Western Europe?*
A: It would indeed. That is exactly what I recommend.

Q: *What, specifically, do you feel is wrong with that strategy?*

A: Today, it is perfectly clear that neither side can initiate a nuclear attack—no matter how limited—without facing the certainty that it will be answered by a nuclear strike in retaliation.

When we declared this doctrine some three decades ago, the U.S. had overwhelming nuclear superiority, Soviet retaliation was questionable. Today, it is no longer in question. The Russians won't blink.

Q: *How do you respond to critics, such as Secretary of State Alexander Haig, who claim that this move would surrender the military advantage in Europe to vastly larger Soviet conventional forces?*

A: Basically, we have overrated the dimensions of this threat. What really counts is *not* the total forces that are available to the Atlantic Alliance and the Warsaw Pact, which seems to give the Soviets a massive edge.

The truly significant factor is the level of forces that two superpowers and their German allies maintain in the center of Europe—in and around Germany. I recognize that, even there, what we have in the field is not sufficient. But the imbalances are not as great as is commonly supposed.

So it is not beyond the realm of possibility that the West could put up a conventional defense that would be adequate for all normal purposes of deterrence. America and Western Europe, after all, are superior to the Eastern bloc both in population and economic might. Meeting the Soviet challenge in conventional power is really a question of political will, pure and simple.

Q: *Hasn't the U.S. threat of nuclear escalation served as a credible deterrent to Soviet aggression?*

A: Certainly it is one deterrent—to the extent that we require such a deterrent. But I don't believe that there has been a time since World War II when the Soviet Union planned or desired an assault on Western Europe. With the problems they have had in Eastern Europe, it just has not been a workable option.

I never thought that, were it not for our nuclear threat, Russia would attack our allies.

Q: *Given Russia's huge military buildup, isn't this a dangerous time for the United States to repudiate any element of its defense strategy?*

A: On the contrary, this is a critical time to do it. Nothing could alleviate the dangers of nuclear war more than for us to renounce the option of being the first to go nuclear. After all, if there is no first use of these weapons, there will be no use of them at all.

Q: *Is there any relationship between your proposal for renouncing first use of atomic arms and increasing pressure to freeze the size of superpower nuclear arsenals?*
A: They are distinctly separate concepts, but they are definitely related. Both have a common goal to reduce the enormous dangers inherent in the atomic age and to call a halt to this insane and provocative pilling up of nuclear weapons. The proposals are mutually supportive and of the highest possible importance.

Q: *How would giving up the first-use strategy help bring about an equitable agreement to stabilize or even cut back the level of nuclear armaments?*
A: The fact that the U.S. still reserves the option to strike the first nuclear blow makes Russia unduly suspicious of American intentions and interferes with arms-control negotiations. If we both declare that we won't be the first to use nuclear weapons—and they have repeatedly offered to do this—a far more relaxed atmosphere might emerge in which serious talks about nuclear-arms reductions could take place.

Q: *How do you respond to the Reagan administration's counterargument that Russia will never seriously consider reducing its nuclear forces until it faces the far more unpleasant alternative of a massive U.S. buildup?*
A: The best answer is that events of the past have not substantiated that theory. In the early 1970s, we put multiple warheads on our missiles in hopes of winning nuclear superiority that would force Russia to negotiate on our terms. But the Soviets simply built up their own weaponry. The result is we're worse off today for our efforts.

Besides, who is refusing to negotiate—the Soviet Union or us? We've delayed for over a year, saying that we are still studying the issue. We could sit down with them today, and they would not be all that unreasonable. They recognize as clearly as we do that the arms race is nearing the edge of absurdity.

Q: *Why, then, does Moscow continue to devote massive resources to a strategic buildup at the expense of economic and social development?*
A: It is, I must say, very wrong, very foolish of them. We are quite right to

object to it. But the point we always miss is that the Russians are much more insecure and defensive than we are.

What they have been trying to achieve since the Cuban missile crisis is nuclear equivalence. The figures never are exactly equal, but it is my impression that we have that equivalence today. So I must frankly acknowledge that I don't know why they go on. They are very misguided.

Q: *Do the Soviets continue to view the U.S. as superior in overall military power?*
A: Yes, I think that they do. More important, they feel encircled. There are only about five or six great powers today—most of them arranged around Russia, most of the hostile. Soviet relations with Japan are not satisfactory. We all have watched the open conflict with China. Moving around to the west, Russians see West Germany, the United States and all of the North Atlantic Treaty Organization arrayed against them. This feeds the kind of insecurity that is common to any regime that has no public support and that must rely on bayonets for both its internal and external security.

Q: *Some experts worry that the 1980s will prove to be very dangerous because Moscow will attain a clear military superiority that it will try to exploit for political gain around the world. What do you make of this theory?*
A: First of all, the Soviet Union is not going to attain *usable* superiority. That concept is empty of meaning so long as both sides have these stupendous quantities of long-range nuclear missiles.

Secondly, nobody in his right mind would yield to that kind of threat. It takes two to make an act of nuclear blackmail. Smaller countries than the NATO group have stood up to Soviet demands, and their hands have never been called. Look at Yugoslavia. It has no nuclear weapons. But it hasn't yielded an inch to the Soviets in forty years. Part of my argument against nuclear weapons is that they're almost useless when you get right down to it.

In reality, the truly perilous time will come not when Moscow feels very strong but when it feels very weak. Desperate people behave in a far more foolish and reckless way than those who are riding along quite well. Kremlin leaders are more likely to lash out if they conclude that their authority in Eastern Europe—or over Russia itself—is unraveling.

Q: *How likely is it that the Soviet Union will be forced to loosen its control over Eastern Europe in years ahead?*

A: That is inevitable. What has happened in Poland in recent months is only one aspect of a far broader phenomenon in the Eastern bloc. The political situation that existed before the rise of the Solidarity union movement will never be restored. There has been a basic change in Eastern Europe, and it is one that eventually will affect all the Eastern European satellite countries.

If things go reasonably slowly in Eastern Europe and the changes take place in ways that do not challenge the Soviet Union's prestige too sharply, then there will be a gradual evolution in the East. The satellites can achieve a greater measure of domestic political independence.

Q: *Do you think that Russia would go so far as to permit the reunification of Germany?*
A: That will clearly be the last thing to occur—if the Russians allow it to happen at all. Fear of a reunified Germany, of course, is the main reason they are so nervous about Poland. The Kremlin views its ability to hold a third of Germany outside of any German-American alliance as the most important spoil that it gained in World War II. They view Poland in light of that reality. East Germany is more important to them than Poland, but the Soviet Union demands things of Poland to preserve its grip on East Germany.

Q: *Do you have any hope that the Soviet Union may at some future time evolve into a more open, perhaps less threatening, society?*
A: One might not be inclined to think so when one sees Russia today, because the changes in the thirty years since Stalin died have been so slight and so glacial that it almost seems like Moscow has found a magic formula for the absolutely static society, free from laws of change.

But that is somewhat deceiving. Certainly, changes are going on under the surface. Some of them are identifiable. They are significant and, from the Kremlin's point of view, they are highly unfavorable.

Q: *What do you mean?*
A: Corruption has grown enormously. The shortage of skilled labor is now at a crisis stage. Productivity is very low. Agricultural difficulties are serious. There is great demoralization, drunkenness to an appalling extent and grow-ing absenteeism on the job. Americanization of Soviet youth is on the rise— blue jeans, rock music, that sort of thing. These problems have existed all the way through, but they're growing worse now.

These are very serious symptoms of a genuine crisis in Soviet society. They reflect a virtually total collapse of the emotional appeal of Marxist-Leninist ideology. It is a stale, out-of-date dogma that doesn't appeal to anyone any more. The people are struggling to escape this spiritual and ideological vacuum into which the Kremlin has plunged them. This may eventually bring the Soviet leaders toward a day of reckoning.

Q: With President Leonid Brezhnev apparently near the end of his tenure, are you concerned that his successors might be more inclined to try to defuse problems at home by taking greater risks in foreign affairs?
A: It's impossible to predict. The new team, for the first time, will consist of leaders who do not have their roots in the Stalin and Lenin era. We know very little about how they will respond to the problems that they will face.

But in any case, in this very delicate period when changes are obviously about to take place in the Soviet leadership, the United States should be extremely cautious about the signals we send to these people because it may shape their policies for a long time.

We should make it plain that, if they want a diminution of this nuclear rivalry and tension, we are prepared to negotiate with them and that we're not going to push them against the wall.

A Diplomat at Century's End

Jeff Trimble / 1996

From *U.S. News & World Report*, 11 March 1996.
Copyright © 1996 by U.S. News & World
Report. Reprinted by permission.

For more than six decades, George Kennan—diplomat, scholar and au-
thor—has been a leading figure in U.S.-Soviet relations. In 1947, he authored
the famous "X article" in *Foreign Affairs* advocating "containment" of the Soviet
Union. Kennan, ninety-two, met last week in New York City with *U.S. News*
Assistant Managing Editor Jeff Trimble to discuss his new book, *At a Century's
Ending*. Excerpts from the interview:

A tragic century:

The twentieth century is a tragic one in the history of European—including
American—civilization. The First World War was in some ways much worse
than the Second World War. The British, French, Germans, and Russians sacrificed the good and better part of their male youth; they had no capital as
valuable as this, and they destroyed it. The Russian Revolution too was a
product of World War I. And that revolution poisoned relations between the
Russian people and the West for seventy years.

Containment:

When I came back from Moscow [after World War II], I was appalled at
the reaction when I told people that my view of the Soviet leadership was not
very favorable: Their faces fell and many of them—particularly those who had
formerly been enthusiastic Soviet allies—said, "Ah, we see it now: Collaboration is not possible, so therefore another war with Russia is inevitable." Well,

168

I didn't believe that at all. Yes, I wanted to say, this regime that exists in Moscow is still Stalin's, exactly the same people who had made the agreement with Hitler in 1939. Yes, these people represent a very serious problem for us—but one that could be dealt with by means short of war. It was in this sense that I spoke of the need for "containment." But it was interpreted much more as though I had meant there was a military threat, that the Russians wanted to attack Western Europe. This fear was exaggerated. Their troops were exhausted, their supplies were exhausted, their country had been destroyed. They were in no position to start another war.

A renewed Russian threat?

I regard a return to Soviet communism as completely impossible. Even a Communist victory in the June presidential election would not bring as much change as people think it would. Any Russian president is still going to have to deal with the realities of the situation, which militate against any great change in policy. They can inflate their currency in order to pay off the miners and other workers. But if they do that, they're going to lose Western support that they very much need. Also, many, many thousands of smaller concerns in Russia have already been privatized.

NATO expansion:

I'm strongly against the idea of expanding NATO up to the Russian frontiers. That is the one thing I can think of that would really stir up a truly troublesome nationalistic, military reaction in Russia. My goodness, look at our Monroe Doctrine; every great power is sensitive about having its immediate neighbors connected with another great military power.

It is well understood by the Russian government—and it will be understood by any people who come in Yeltsin's place—that any attempt to attack toward the west, say toward Poland, or to bring back Ukraine by force of arms would probably produce another European war. They are not in any position to face that.

U.S. national interests:

We have two great global interests. One is the world environmental crisis—overpopulation, urbanization, and the exhaustion of the world's resources. The second is bringing nuclear weaponry and the weapons of mass destruction under control and, I hope, achieving their total abolition. Besides those, the greatest dangers I see are the ones we present to ourselves, the well-known deficiencies in our own civilization, which we are not facing up to and which obviously our political establishment isn't able to face up to successfully. We need to keep our relations with the rest of the world on an even keel, protecting ourselves against the competitive forces that are mobilized against us while putting our own country on a sound basis.

Diplomacy:

I see no diminution in the need for a really good diplomatic apparatus. But our whole diplomatic apparatus is vastly overbureaucratized today. Diplomacy is basically the responsibility of the president and the secretary of state, and they've allowed far too much of it to slip into other semi-independent hands. Washington needs a housecleaning.

Index